Praise for *Magical Trees*

"*Magical Trees* will ignite your imagination and provide a bridge for more deeply understanding and relating to the natural magic of the world of trees. You'll find yourself inspired and enlightened as to how these incredible beings bring so much to this world and will learn creative ways to connect and collaborate with their magic. After reading this book you'll never look at another tree in the same way!"

—Dr. Steven Farmer, author of *Earth Magic, Earth Magic Oracle Cards*, and *Messages from the Spirits of Nature Oracle Cards*. www.drstevenfarmer.com

"If you've ever sensed that trees have magic, if you've ever felt drawn to certain trees, or if you simply enjoy sitting with your back up against a sturdy tree trunk, then this is the book for you. Discover the power of trees in Kac Young's *Magical Trees*. Dr. Young offers a master class on meeting, understanding, connecting with, respecting, and loving trees, leading a guided tour of their vibrant history and mythology and teaching you how to discover, honor, and harness their magic. This is a book that is not only needed, but long overdue. In *Magical Trees*, Dr. Young takes you on a journey deep into the soul of trees that will forever change how you view and interact with them."

—Karen Frazier, author, energy healer, and psychic medium

"Kac Young speaks fluent Tree—a delicious language, and one that holds the potential to transform our relationships not just with trees but with all life, including ourselves. Taking us gently by the hand, Young guides us to approach a tree with reverence, request permission to commune, open our inner ears, and listen, perhaps for the first time, to an ancient voice that wants to be heard. What will you hear? Ah, therein lies deep magic."

—Janet Conner, prayer artist, mystic witch, author of *Writing Down Your Soul, The Lotus and the Lily* and m̶o̶r̶e̶

"Author Kac Young has done it again with her latest book, *Magical Trees: A Guidebook for Finding the Magic in Everyday Trees, Using Crystals, Spells, Essential Oils, and Rituals*. She poses the question, 'What do trees mean to you?' The answer should be, 'everything,' as they are the lungs of our planet. Kac Young reminds us of the magical language of trees. Trees speak to us all the time, and this is one of the first books that shares their enchanting language. Trees teach us that even with the smallest act of kindness and care for nature we are making a big difference. I know personally when I am in the presence of a great oak I am in awe of her magnificence. This delightful book is for anyone who has ever had a strong affinity to trees and can feel their heart and soul when in their presence. Everything has consciousness, including our beloved trees. Young guides us on how to work with our favorite trees and tap into the tree's powerful energetic field for healing both inside and out."

—Melisa Caprio, author of *Postcards to the Universe: Harness the Universe's Power and Manifest Your Dreams*

"In Kac Young's *Magical Trees*, you will find all the ritual and spiritual tools to connect with the magic of the trees all around us. She enlightens newcomers with the deep, ancient wisdom trees hold and allows those of us who already have a deep connection to reach even further into our spiritual practice to connect with the truth of trees. They are the oldest and most profound magic found in this world whose mystical power we must learn to protect and acknowledge with reverence. Enter a sacred, reciprocal bond that will lend the healing you need, the knowledge you seek and open your spirit to a world beyond the physical plane we see."

—Cerridwen Greenleaf, author of *The Herbal Healing Handbook*

Magical Trees

Magical Trees

A GUIDEBOOK FOR FINDING THE MAGIC IN EVERYDAY TREES USING CRYSTALS, SPELLS, ESSENTIAL OILS, AND RITUALS

KAC YOUNG, PhD, ND, DCH

CORAL GABLES

For permission requests, please contact the publisher at:

Mango Publishing Group

2850 S Douglas Road, 4th Floor

Coral Gables, FL 33134 USA

info@mango.bz

For special orders, quantity sales, course adoptions and corporate sales, please email the publisher at sales@mango.bz. For trade and wholesale sales, please contact Ingram Publisher Services at customer.service@ingramcontent.com or +1.800.509.4887.

Magical Trees: A Guidebook for Finding the Magic in Everyday Trees using Crystals, Spells, Essential Oils, and Rituals

Library of Congress Cataloging-in-Publication number: 2021951824

ISBN: (print) 978-1-64250-774-4, (ebook) 978-1-64250-775-1

BISAC category code OCC028000, BODY, MIND & SPIRIT / Magick Studies

Printed in the United States of America

+ + +

To General Sherman at Henry Cowell Redwoods State Park
My beloved limon tree from Guadalajara
Helen Keller Squirrel's Favorite Oak in Cambria, California
Brenda Knight for asking me to write this book

+ + +

Contents

Foreword

Several years ago, I accidentally realized that nature speaks to us when I discovered the healing properties of colored gems after several of my colored stones began telling me what they would do, how they work, and so forth. Sometime later, I distinctly recall trees speaking to me in a similar manner. The messages were similar to stones, and the trees wanted me to know that they too can do different things energetically. Because I immersed myself in the study of gems and writing about them, I never got around to following up on the messages the trees wanted to send. I'm pleased to report that Kac Young heard the call, and I'm so happy she answered!

Trees are magical helpers who cleanse our environment, but they're also trusted advisors, filled with the wisdom of the ages if we care to listen.

I'm sure we can all agree that our planet is in dire need of healing at this time. Our environment is of paramount concern these days. Activists speak of the dire need for us to focus on pressing issues such as air quality, assisting endangered species, and protecting land—all of which are keenly important for humanity to survive. But what about our trees? Kac Young's brilliant deep dive into the wonders of our other earthly cohabitants helps us remember that our trees should be a huge part of the conservation conversation.

Not only must we shift our current habits and consciousness to care for the air quality and environment itself to sustain life here, but the other beings also who coinhabit our earth urgently need our attentive love and care.

We must love and appreciate each other like never before. While we usually consider human beings at the top of our list of who we need to cherish, many also include animals, which is a good thing. Still, it's important to pause to consider the trees by acknowledging that they too are sentient beings who share our earth and our space and deserve our respect like people and animals.

Kac's personification of our fellow inhabitants of Earth reminds us to consider these treasured kindred spirits by understanding their historical backgrounds. Just as we should do with our fellow human beings, after learning the rich history of trees, we all emerge with deeper understanding and commitment to do what it takes to preserve and protect those who have lived on this planet far longer than we have so they may be here in force for future generations.

Because so many trees have been on the planet far longer than any human, we must somehow learn from them and hear the wisdom and ideas I know for a fact they long to share with us. That's where *Magical Trees* comes in as our helpful assistant. Kac Young gives readers a shortcut to understanding the beautiful depths of the souls of our beloved trees. Kac's incredible historical accounts and antidotes help seekers get to the heart of tree consciousness and help us know and understand these incredible tree beings in ways we may not have considered before. The personification of their personalities makes trees approachable and helps us strengthen our bond through familiarity and friendship. She also teaches readers how to use other spiritual tools such as oils and crystals to enhance the tree's messages to begin forming the lasting bond of friendship that will inspire us all to make a steadfast effort toward the sustainable planet we all hope to create. Open your minds and your hearts and allow the trees to assist you in expanding your awareness and happiness in life, and above all, enjoy the Magical Trees!

—Shelley A. Kaehr, PhD, author of *Past Lives with Pets* and
Heal Your Ancestors to Heal Your Life

Introduction

Trees were here on Earth long before humans and most creatures. They come in every shape and size and are known to take a human's breath away with their seasonal display of vibrant and electrifying colors. Some trees flower and create aromas that waft through the forest or your backyard, transporting you to another world. Some grow thorns to protect themselves against invaders or destroyers; others provide food in the form of fruits, berries, nuts, or nourishing sap. Each one is incredibly magnificent and uniquely reflects the environment of its origin. Trees are home to creatures, fairies, hummingbirds, bees, squirrels, and millions of insects and algae, as well as moss and lichens that we cannot live without.

Throughout the ages, civilizations have used trees to represent gods, myths, legends, rituals, creation stories, and oracles. They have been celebrated as symbols for the stages of life, sources of wisdom, fertility, examples of power, and even as shelter from the elements for humans and animals. Many ancient cultures relied on trees for their refuge and safety and even climbed them as natural ladders to avert danger or imminent death.

Philosophers attribute trees as observers of the evolution of humanity and witnesses to the progression of the planet around them. Ascended Masters claim they are the soul of the earth and hold ancient wisdom. The day we learn that about trees, our lives change.

> The term "ascended master" initially was used by Baird T. Spalding in his series of books, *Life and Teachings of the Masters of the Far East* (DeVorss and Co.). They are referred to as beings who have once been incarnated as human but now exist in the fifth and sixth dimensions and hold the wisdom of the ages.

Trees have been many things to many civilizations. A grove of trees might have been deemed sacred, with rituals and ceremonies conducted, often in secret, within the protective enclave of branches and trunks. Rich history and fascinating lore lives within the simple yet complex tree.

We are about to begin a journey to find and reveal the magic in trees, learn how they came to have been granted stature, and explore how we can use their magical power for our lives and community.

What do trees mean to you? If you say "nothing," then you are about to embark upon the ride of your life. By the end of this book, I promise that you will not only understand the basic common trees, but you will learn to love them with all your heart. Maybe you said, "Everything," then you probably have had a wonderful experience with a tree—something that you remember and cherish about a particular tree and the time in your life that brought you both together. Great. Then, you are already a convert, and you're guaranteed to love this book.

In the following chapters we will read a little bit about trees throughout history, then we'll venture into what other civilizations thought about trees and what they used them for in their lives. We'll explore the sacred aspects of trees from Norse, Germanic, Celtic, Greek, Indian, South American, Asian, and American Indian lore, medicine, and beliefs. Together, we'll discover a tree's poetic nature, heart, and soul and exciting presence within.

Coming up, we'll learn about the holy days of trees, world-famous trees, working trees, tree spirits, how to read a tree, and, most importantly, how to find the magic in trees. We'll learn about the special powers a tree possesses and why they are so incredibly important not just to our lives, but also to our souls.

Certain etiquettes are required to find these magical trees and appropriate ways to introduce yourself to them. We have so much to learn from a tree! I'm dying to tell you more about what I have discovered.

Welcome to the journey of *Magical Trees: A Guidebook for Finding the Magic in Everyday Trees, Using Crystals, Spells, Essential Oils, and Rituals.*

I fervently wish that you enjoy every page of this book and become a metaphysical expert and spiritual authority in the enchanting world of trees and why we literally can't live without them.

Chapter One

What Are Magical Trees?

What *are* Magical Trees, and how would you recognize one if you saw it? There is no quick and easy answer, but this chapter is dedicated to investigating that question and much more.

If you are a history buff, you know many cultures worship trees—especially the Celtic culture. Read on because, according to research from the University of California at Berkeley, trees have an almost undetectable magnetic field of energy that surrounds them. For years, they have been searching for biomagnetism in plants using some of the most sensitive magnetic detectors available. They faced a few problems, like interference from other magnetic fields of traffic on land, air, and subterranean "noise." When they were able to bore through those signals, they discovered that trees only gave off one-millionth of the electromagnetism given by the earth's field. But that's still something.

One of the researchers, Eric Corsini, said they were disappointed in not being able to measure electromagnetism more thoroughly "because we couldn't find a way to cancel out the local ambient magnetic field noise" (Sanders 2011). What is solidly true is that they may not have had the instrumentation at that time to detect the electromagnetic fields of trees, but we *can* measure what damage electromagnetic radiation, especially from cell phone transmitters, does to trees.

In animals, for example, activity in the heart and brain produces tiny magnetic fields that sensitive magnetometers can measure. Trees do give off something; perhaps we don't have the right kind of instruments to measure what they exude, or maybe we are looking in the wrong places. Just because we don't have the equipment to detect it doesn't mean it isn't there. The electromagnetic fields of trees are present differently than we understand. In time, a measurement device will be created, and we'll all sit back and say, "There it is!"

Why does this matter? Because humans have an electromagnetic field, and that electromagnetic field interacts with the electromagnetic field of the tree, creating a third field. This is how we exchange, feel, and use the energy and the magic from the tree.

This is how a scientist defines it. Jack Fraser, University of Oxford, department of physics, says, "You *are* an electric field—a giant electric field which holds your atoms together, and which uses other electric fields to talk to other bits of yourself. Every atom has its own electric field, and when you put two atoms close together, they can mess around with the electric field of the other" (Fraser 2017).

The magic exists in the third field created between you and the tree. This field, created by your energy and the tree's energy, contains the objective power—call it a vibration, electromagnetism, energy field, power, conjuring, divination, sorcery, or spell, to turn your intentions and dreams into reality. Add in the advancement of scalar energy, the energy that Nikola Tesla was going to use to create telecommunication signals, and we can use the energy of a tree from a distance without wires. Scalar energy are circles of energy that radiate outward in a balanced network of energy stems that are alive. On the practical level, this means that you can connect with trees from far, far away. Use any means you wish, but consciously engage with the tree, and you can enjoy its magic.

Moving further into the subject, now that we know a tree has magic, is to learn how we go about working with it. It is true; some trees may have a little more magic than others. And it may be that some trees interact with different human energies than others, but there is magic to be discerned in every tree. You'll have to sharpen your *treedar* to discover which trees work with you and for you. Let's get deeper into the process step by step.

How to Approach a Tree

Use the variety of guidebooks and available material to help you identify the trees. I mean, you wouldn't want to hurt a tree's feelings by mistaking an oak for an elm, would you? Pinterest has a lot of great one-sheet tree, bark and leaf or needle identifying reference material. I use them all the time.

Each tree has four levels of magic to consider. There is *Leaf or Needle Magic*; *Branch Magic*; *Root Magic*; and *Whole Tree Magic*, with each part of the tree different magical qualities are attached.

Magical Part	Magical Qualities
Leaf or Needle	Transformation, Alchemy, Giving, and Releasing
Branch	Growth, Strength, Embracing, Reaching
Root	Support, Grounding, Connection, Depth
Whole Tree	Power, Endurance, Longevity, Steadfastness

Leaf or Needle Magic; Branch Magic; Root Magic; and Whole Tree Magic.

When you know what you want and how you want to incorporate a tree's magic into your process, then you will know which parts of the tree can help you the most.

1. Locate the tree (type) you want to work with. Certain trees grow in certain areas, so you will want to make sure you research your geographical tree regions. When you find the tree you want to work with, follow these guidelines.

2. You want to establish a rapport with your chosen tree. Attune yourself to it by first having a thorough look at it. Take in all the details about the tree, its size, girth, leaves, branches, shape, color, and shape. Approach the tree to check if you can *feel* it. (I always like to ask permission before I enter its space. When I sense that permission has been granted, I approach with dignity. I may lean up against the tree to sense its heartwood. I may embrace it gently for the same reason.)

3. Remain curious about a tree, as if it were the first time you have seen it. Notice little things about the tree, who lives in it or on it, and get a sense if there is a spirit or a fairy that lives within.

4. Close your eyes and deeply connect with the tree. You might take a leaf or a branch in your hands and use your senses to intake what the tree has to offer. (Sometimes, I'll go so far as to sense what it would like to be this tree. How would that feel?)

5. By this time, you feel you have become a friend to this tree, and the next thing you might do is ask its permission to take some leaves, needles, fruit, nuts, seeds, or maybe a branch. Never want to cause damage to your tree. Interact with the tree to see what is acceptable. (If I am given the okay to take a branch, I always use a sharp tool that I have cleaned to keep the tree from disease, bacteria, or fungi, and I lop off what I have been allowed. I carry pruning sealant with me to wipe on the wound since I have made the tree vulnerable with my cut, and I want to clean the cut and seal it to protect it from insects and invaders. If I am picking fruit, berries, nuts, or seeds, the same guidelines and permissions apply.)

6. Leave some tobacco sprinkled around the tree in gratitude for the gift it has given you. Thank the tree and leave knowing that you have been a reciprocal friend and left something in exchange for what you have taken.

7. If you have extra time, stay with the tree for a while, have a refreshment, read a book, listen to music, and share your time with the tree. (Sometimes I'll ask it if it needs anything. Trees have a lovely way of giving you an answer.)

8. If you take a picture of a tree so you can work with its magic later, be sure to ask permission. The spirits in the trees need to give you permission before you snap away. You wouldn't want someone taking random pictures of your house, would you? Always be respectful, and you will have a glorious relationship with the trees.

Sometimes it may take you a while to find a tree that you relate to as magical. Trees are wise and able to sense who you are and what intentions you have. Trees sing, their branches can moan in the wind, the leaves can crackle and rattle, the tree can sway and bend if the wind is strong enough. Be sure to listen to what they have to say while you are in their presence.

When you have found your tree and connected, be aware of the special healing field the two of you have created together. You may want to use this field for healing on the spot. You may want to charge up healing crystals in this energy. You may want to do the same with essential oils, talismans, amulets, or a wand. Your time with the tree is sacred and charged with beautiful energy. When you part ways with the tree, you will leave with your electromagnetic energy field, the tree will remain with its field, and the third field you created together will dissipate. I like to capture that energy in crystals I have with me that I have pre-programmed to receive it. This way, I keep the healing field close by, wherever I need to call on it.

If you have a set of wooden Ogham, take them with you on tree visits. They will feel right at home and serve you well. (See Chapter Five.)

Magical trees are everywhere. They could be in your backyard, in a park, along your street, in your apartment complex, at the office. Keeping a journal about the trees you meet is a wonderful way to break into identifying them and knowing who they are, what qualities they have, and how they can share their gifts with you for your magical life. Sketching trees is also a wonderful way to capture an image of them and take it with you. Even if you don't work magic, your life is still magical and filled with the ability to connect with the magic trees and their astonishing gifts.

Drawing Magic from a Tree: A Ritual

When I first began to discover the magical qualities of trees, I wasn't sure how to know which ones were magical and which ones were not. I discovered that all trees have *degrees* of magic in them. It was up to me to find out which ones did and how much magic they had. Sometimes you need powerful magic, and sometimes you need a gentle hint.

I devised a ten-step ritual that would allow me to access the magical qualities of each tree so I would learn more about its talents. If you want to discover the magic in trees, you can try out my ritual if you like.

Ten-Step Ritual for Assessing the Magic in a Tree

1. Find a tree that appeals to you from the heart. Stand beside it. Ask permission of the tree to connect with it. Ask it if it will share its essence with you. Be sure to confirm that you mean no harm. Find something from the tree that has fallen—a leaf, a piece of bark, a seed, a cone, a branch, a twig, and take it into your hands. Close your eyes and concentrate deeply on what you have in your hand. Feel the texture, experience the weight, note the temperature—does it speak to you somehow? Can you feel the life in it? Does it have a scent?

2. Open your eyes after connecting with the piece of the tree. Observe the entire tree. Walk around it. Look into the ground to visualize the roots, observe the bark or covering. Gauge how deep that bark or covering is. Gaze intently at the leaves, twigs, needles, branches. Is the tree symmetrical, asymmetrical, twisted, straight, gnarled? Now, pay attention to the colors in all the parts of the tree. In your mind, label the colors, use colorful adjectives, and try to describe the tree in as many poetic terms as you can.

3. Now that you have a picture of the tree, close your eyes and recreate the tree in your imagination. Add its aroma into the scenario and begin to *feel* the tree's inner life. Don't open your eyes yet. Answer these questions: Is the tree male or female in your feelings? What element comes to mind when you tune into the kinesthetics of the tree? What else can you sense about the tree? Do you hear music? Birds? Other sounds?

4. If you have a sense of the tree's qualities, you may open your eyes and begin to write them down. At this point, I like to engage in a spoken dialog with the tree. I'll say something like, "I'm sensing that your magic is protection, would that be correct?" Or "I feel you have a nurturing spirit. Am I on the right track?" "Are you able to communicate with the fairies? The other world?" "Is there a spirit that lives within you?" "May I know their name(s)?" "Are you a tree of love?" "Can your magic bring long life?" "Would you say you are a tree of good fortune?" "Does your magic purify and cleanse?" Keep asking positive questions until you get a sense of the tree's purpose and what it enjoys doing. If you remain open and in this meditative state, the tree will let you know the answers.

5. At the end of your conversation with the tree, ask how you can be of service to it. I like to ask if it is afraid of anything. Once a tree told me, "Rodents," so I wrapped a slick tube of aluminum around the

trunk that the rodents couldn't climb. It seemed to be much happier and produced a wonderful crop that year.

6. I have been known to tell the tree about all the good things being done in the world to help trees. I have brought a bag of nutrients for a tree if it is fading, and, occasionally, if I revisit the tree, I might tell it about the products that we make from it and how they help people. Trees love you to engage in chat with them. There are opportunities to bring songs for the tree if you are so inclined and a gift that it might enjoy. I have given them tobacco as a token of the earth, crystals from the ground, stones from other places, and even a sack full of ladybugs to help with chomping insects.

7. Before I leave, I spend time thanking the tree. I ask if I may have some products from the tree—leaves, needles, cones, branches, etc. The answer is often yes, but if the tree says no, I leave it alone. Something is going on. You will know what to do. Usually, I ask for permission to take a photo or sketch the tree, and I make sure the tree is compensated for its time spent with me by my gratitude and my little gifts.

8. I take time to make notes so I don't forget what the tree and I discussed. I'll usually ask if I can return. Sometimes I read my poem to it, the one at the end of Chapter Nine. I haven't met a tree yet that didn't appreciate those words.

9. When I return home, I have a special altar where I place my tree souvenirs. They remind me of the precious time I spent with that tree, the connection we had, and the confirmation of my questions, so I can cherish a deeper sense of what magic the tree holds.

10. I keep a file on which trees have what magic. I can go back to them when I need assistance with those qualities. If I have asked for and taken gifts from the tree, I can enlist those for ritual practice or when I need to use some of what they have to share. I mentioned in a previous chapter that I frequently take along crystals that I have programmed to receive the tree's energy and attributes. The crystals retain the tree's energy, and I can call upon that when I need it, along with the souvenirs I have taken away with me. (A list of compatible crystals for each tree is in the Reference section at the back of the book.)

Trees are full of life and power. I come to them in a spirit of respect and, oftentimes, awe. For me, it is a privilege to connect with them and with nature. I always feel enlightened and uplifted by our interaction. I'm sure you will make up your ritual for finding the magic in trees. This ritual might be just a beginning for you. I hope it is and that you will continue to explore what the trees have to say and share.

Not only are trees magical, but other cultures long before us have deemed some of them sacred and holy. In the next chapter, we will meet some of those special and honorable trees and find out why they are so special.

Chapter Two

Sacred Trees in History, Religion, and Mythology

In this chapter, we will get to know the famous, sacred trees of the cultures that preceded us. You might be thinking, "Why do we care?" We care because they set the precedents of how we currently view trees today, why they were respected in the past, and how that affects us, even today, in our outlook and interaction with the tree community. The names may look foreign to us, so I won't name them all in this introductory paragraph. They are listed in alphabetical order and may surprise you with their histories, differences, and similarities. Remember, the myths surrounding these trees emanated from divergent cultures around the globe long before there were easy channels of communication for sharing ideas. Many cultures designated a tree as their central symbol to explain creation. See how much you agree with as you read along.

Ağaç Ana

The early Turks practiced Buddhism, Christianity, Judaism, and Manichaeism before converting to Islam. Hence, they had a deep and varied scope of mysticism.

Ağaç Ana was regarded as the mother of creation. The Altai Turks believed human beings are virtually descended from trees. According to the legends of the Yakuts, White Mother sits at the base of the Tree of Life, whose branches reach to the heavens. In the heavens, they are occupied by many supernatural creatures that have come to life there. The blue sky surrounding the tree indicates the peaceful nature of the upper world country. The red ring surrounding all the elements represents the ancient faith of rebirth, growth, and development of the Turkic peoples (Sproul 1979). Though the tree is not present, today, the Ağaç Ana is now a toy store in Turkey where wooden children's toys are made.

Ashvattha

Ashvattha (*Ficus religiosa*) in Hindu mythology refers to the tree under which the Buddha, Siddhartha Gautama, sat for forty-nine nights and achieved enlightenment. It is also called the Bodhidruma, meaning *tree of supreme spiritual enlightenment*, and is in Bodh Gaya, Bihar, India.

The Bodhi Tree is called Ashvattha.

The Peepal, or *Ficus religiosa*, is super sacred. According to legendary belief, Lord Vishnu and other gods resided under it. Hindus worship the Peepal because they believe that this tree represents various gods and goddesses like Vishnu, Buddha, Krishna, Brahma, Lakshmi, Surya, Aditya, and Vana Durga, to mention a few. Many women worship the Peepal to avoid widowhood and spinsterhood.

To the Upanishad culture, the fruit of the Peepal is used to explain the difference between the body and the soul: the body is like the fruit which, being outside, feels and enjoys things, while the soul is like the seed, which is inside and therefore witnesses things (Nagar 2021).

Sadly, the original tree met with a violent death. It was hacked down by the cruel ruler Pushyamitra Sanga of the Mauryan Empire in the second century BCE. He persecuted Buddhists and destroyed their main symbol and sacred tree, The Tree of Knowledge. However, every time he cut the tree down, a new tree was planted in its place.

Because, during the reign of Ashoka the Great, a branch of this Bodhi tree had been taken to Sri Lanka and transplanted there. King Ashoka's daughter planted the original shoot from the Bodhi tree in Sri Lanka in the third century BCE. The Bodhi Tree flourishes today with no signs of ageing at the Mahavihara Theravada Buddhism monastery in Anuradhapura (Mehrotra 2017).

Egig érő fa

From Hungary and some of its geographical neighbors like Germany, Croatia, Serbia, Bulgaria, Turkey, and Transylvania, there are slightly modified versions of the same myth. Generally, though, the main myth surrounding the tree *égig érő fa* retains its similarities.

According to the myth of the *égig érő fa*, the existence of The World Tree is divided into three levels. The first world is the Upper World (Felső világ), where the gods and advanced spirits live. The major celestial bodies (the Sun and the Moon) are also located in the Upper World. The sky is believed to be a large tent held up by the Tree of Life. Many little holes in the tent ceiling are the stars.

The second level is the Middle World (Középső világ), where humans, animals, plants, and trees live. The Middle World is also shared with mythological creatures who are often supernatural. There are ghosts of the forests and waters, who have been told to scare humans. There are females, the *sellő* (mermaid), which live in water and have a human torso with the tail of a fish. The wind is controlled by an old lady called *Szélanya* (Wind Mother) or *Szélkirály* (Wind King).

The third level is the Underworld (Alsó világ), where the demons and evil spirits dwell. The underworld is the home of Ördög, creator of everything bad for humans, like fleas, lice, and flies. It is not established whether the underworld was regarded as a place of punishment since its naming as Pokol (Hell) developed after the birth of Christianity.

Its name, égig érő fa, means *sky high tree*, and this tree grows right in the middle of all three worlds like a pole holding them up, connecting them and giving them continuity and connection.

Its other names are életfa, meaning *tree of life*, világfa meaning *World Tree*, and tetejetlen fa, meaning *tree without a top*.

The fable states that only the *táltosok* (shamans) were allowed to climb the égig érő fa because they had the proper knowledge to understand the realms and explore the seven to nine layers of the sky. Tengrism, a shamanic religion common among the early Turkic and Mongolian people, featured this worldview.

Egig érő fa was both honored and feared because if an ordinary human dared to approach it, all hell would break loose. The tree was believed to have its top in heaven and its roots in hell. Frequently hawks or the mythical bird known as Turul would sit on its branches.

Variations of the myth came from other countries and involved a story about a shepherd who climbed the tree to save a princess held against her will by a dragon, and a series of humorous tales about a gypsy who climbed his way to heaven and ended up in hell. It was a generational privilege to make up your own myth about égig érő fa and hand it down to the next generation. There are many versions out in the world of this famous tree, and everyone from that part of the world may tell you a different tale.

Modun, Eeg Mod

Samoyed mythology believed that the world tree connects different realities of human spiritual experience. The underworld, this world, the middle world, and the upper world are all connected by the central tree. Their mythology holds that the world tree is also the symbol of Mother Earth, who is said to bestow his drum on the Samoyed shaman, which enabled him to travel from one world to another, Upper, Middle, and Under.

Today, Eej Mod, The Mother Tree, is still celebrated annually by the Shaman culture. Many Mongolian families have their own Shaman who helps them communicate between the spirits of family members, alive and deceased. This annual celebration happens around the tree and involves food, vodka, milk, and encircling the tree for chants, prayers, and praise.

The beliefs of the shamanic celebrants centered on a fear of nature and a belief that Shamans could control the good and evil spirits. The celebrants become one with the tree by putting their heads through a hole in the old tree and making wishes. There is a mix of Buddhism and Shamanism in Mongolia. The original Mother Tree was burned during the communist revolution and an eminent Shaman proclaimed a nearby tree Eej Mod. This tree is visited and celebrated by believers in Mongolia (Notes: Eej Mod Mother Tree 2021).

> Many ancient sacred trees were divided into three worlds: The Upper World, The Middle World, and The Lower World.

Irminsul

Irminsul was a tree located at the center of a pagan place of sacrifice and worship in the ancient Germanic world. There has been no real proof that such a place existed, but oral history referred to Irmin as a god.

Legend has it that Irminsul, the place, received its name from the Germanic god Irmin, whose name meant *great, strong, tall.*

According to another legend, Charlemagne came thundering through the area conquering Saxony in the eighth century, and, according to the Royal Frankish Annals, ordered the destruction of Irminsul, the chief seat of the (pagan) Saxon religion. Irminsul is linked to the philosophy of Yggdrasil and the god Odin.

The location of Irminsul is still a debated topic, but it appears as if this sacred place was in the vicinity of Heresburg (now Obermarsberg), Germany. After Imrminsul was destroyed, it was replaced by a stone structure (Lloyd 2019).

Iroko

The Iroko is a large hardwood tree grown in Southern Nigeria, Ghana, Guinea, Angola, Benin, and Mozambique. It is also known as logo and loko to the Yoruba people and has immense significance as a sacred and magical tree. In Africa, it is common for people to worship the trees and the forests. Three African groups that worship trees are the Yoruba, the Olukomi, and the Voodun.

There is a generational belief that the spirits of their ancestors live on through the trees. To pay special homage, the sacred trees are highly manicured and some even sculpted into a design. Most of all, they provide a sheltered place where communities can gather and hold their dances, rituals, and tribal sessions. In some religions, sacred trees are also thought to have magical powers that can chastise, cure, or work miracles.

The Iroko tree is commercially known as African teak, but it is unrelated to the teak family. Iroko is widely used in herbal medicine. The bark treats coughs and heart problems. If one is cured by the tree, it is thought to be a magical deed.

The Yoruba people believe that the Iroko tree is inhabited by a spirit called the Iroko-man. Anyone who stands face-to-face with the Iroko-man becomes insane and quickly perishes. Anyone who tries to cut down the Iroko tree will be besotted by great misfortune unless they pray for protection. One example is that a five-hundred-year-old tree was cut down in the past, and the families fled because of the suffering they experienced (Thorogood Timber Merchant 2021).

> The Iroko tree is inhabited by a spirit called Iroko-man. Anyone who stands face-to-face with Iroko-man becomes insane and quickly perishes.

African legend says that Iroko lives at the top of the tree in its canopy. The limbs reach so high into the sky that it is considered the throne of God. Spirits live within the tree and are assigned to keeping Iroko from descending to earth. On a quiet night, it is said that the cries of the Iroko man can be heard throughout the land.

Kien-Mu or Jian-Mu

Kien-Mu or Jian-Mu, the Chinese World Tree, was a complex representation of life for the ancients. There are three worlds of Kien-Mu, and they all contain the representations of yin and yang, light and dark, day and night, east and west.

The first world, the Celestial World

The moon and sun are represented on opposite sides. The crow raises the sun, and the hare is linked to the night in company with the toad.

At the base of the celestial world, two characters, assisted by two ferocious dragons, prevent access to the celestial gates to those considered unworthy.

The second world, the Terrestrial World

Yang and yin are intimately linked, and the dead must cross the obscure world before attaining light.

The third world, the Underground (and water) World

Two dragons living in the terrestrial world have tails that are entangled in the world below. They are reminders that our roots are interlinked, and no one escapes the depths where yin and yang also abide.

At the deepest part of the underground world, two intertwined fish, representing yin and yang, turn toward the west and the east. It is from this world that the world tree draws its nourishment and source of life.

The tree and the journey are far more intricate than what I have explained here, but it would take a good deal of time to read and understand the elaborate symbolic representations of the images within the Chinese world tree.

Yaxche

Yaxche is the tree of life for the Maya. Traditionally a Ceiba tree, it features a straight trunk and has large, buttressed roots. It grows tall with a high horizontal crown. The roots are believed to shelter bats, symbols of the underworld. The trunk is home to insects and the birds that feed on them. The crown spreads majestically like a canopy showing four branches representing the four cardinal directions in Mayan astrology. Eagles roost on the treetop to suggest the presence of the celestial realm.

The tree's center is called the *axis mundi* and is believed to be the navel of the world. A Yaxche tree was planted at the center of most pre-Colombian Mesoamerican villages. It complimented the Mayan temple, a vertical structure designed to replicate the passage from the subterranean to the heavenly realms.

The Tree of Life motif is also commonly found as a design element in highland Maya textiles (Buried Mirror Yaxche Tree 2021).

Yggdrasil

In Norse mythology, Yggdrasil is an enormous ash tree that is the holy tree of the North. In the thirteenth century, the Poetic Edda and the Prose Edda described the sacred tree that explains spiritual belief and the characters and levels of the ancient myths. There are both regions and seasons connected by the tree.

Yggdrasil translated means *Odin's horse. Ygg* is another name for the god Odin. *Drasill* means *horse*. Additionally, *drasill* also means *walker* or *pioneer*. In some sections of the manuscript, Yggdrasil and Odin appear interchangeable.

Odin is said to have hung on the tree upside down and lanced with a spear for nine days. (Nine worlds are portrayed by Yggdrasil.) Odin came out of the ordeal enlightened. The poetry indicates that Odin and the tree are one, and all three layers blend into one and grow out of the same root.

The Norns, three wise women, are the protectors and guardians of Yggdrasil. The Norns weave on a loom which represents time itself. They represent Urd (past), Verdandi (present), and Skuld (future).

In Norse creation myths, men and women originated from trees, and they believe we are all sons and daughters of the ash and elm trees. The first man was Ask, born from ash, and the first woman Embla, born from the elm. Ask and Embla sprouted from Yggdrasil's acorns; therefore, every subsequent human has sprung from the fruit of Yggdrasil.

Artur Lundkvist, one of Swedish literature's greatest tree worshippers, said this about trees.

"…in every human there is a tree, and in every tree, there is a human, I feel this, the tree wonders inside a human being, and the human being is caught in the tree" (Kornevall 2017).

Many Northerners entranced by Yggdrasil planted a miniature version of Yggdrasil in the center of their homes. It is also known as the care tree and represents the interdependence of humans and the world(s) around them. It may have been the forerunner to the Christmas tree in the West.

The World Tree Yggdrasil is important because it is connected to our own creation story, preservation, and destruction. It teaches us that trees are bound to the fate of the earth. It is important that we care for our past and remember what we have lost, and it reminds us to celebrate the flowering energy of the world, the present moment, at the same time we are reaching forward toward a new and brighter future (Kornevall 2017).

> Yggdrasil teaches us that trees are bound to the fate of the earth.

Of course, many other trees and plants were sacred, and that information would fill another book entirely. I wanted to share a brief overview of some of the world's most famous, sacred trees along with the cosmological beliefs they represented for ancient cultures.

In the next chapter, we'll look at some of the oldest trees in the world. Each of them is uniquely amazing.

Chapter Three

The Oldest Trees in the World

In human terms, making it to a hundred years old is a great feat. But imagine being a tree and living a hundred times older than that. Here are some stories I found about the oldest trees in the world. There might be something we can learn from them.

Trees are amazing storehouses of ancient wisdom and the keepers of the earth's soul. One discovery of an ancient tree preserved in New Zealand revealed that Earth's magnetic field flipped some 42,000 years ago, termed the *Laschamp Excursion*. The 1,700-year-old tree, known by its Maori name *Kauri*, was perfectly preserved, and scientists read the detailed measurements in a radioactive form of carbon throughout the tree rings. How the rings were formed led them to determine that a radical climate change occurred due to a switch in polar activity 42,000 years ago (Gerhard 2019). This information and carbon-dated age help us today as we experience climate change once again.

Trees are dated using two methods: *dendrochronology*, a scientific method of dating the annual growth rings of a tree, which is regarded as accurate, and *radiocarbon dating*, used for older trees, which determines date-ranges rather than a specific age in years. Radiocarbon dating told us Kauri was alive 42,000 years ago.

The Ten Oldest Trees in the World

Number Ten

The Senator, a Pond Cypress (*Taxodium ascendens*), was a 3,500-year-old tree that was accidentally burned down in 2012. Its demise was tragic and horribly sad. It was in Longwood, Florida, and regally stood 118 feet tall. The top had been damaged by a hurricane in 1925, but it recovered and thrived for another eighty years.

If you're curious about the person who burned down the tree, I was too, so I researched the story. Her name was Sara Barnes, and she and a friend were smoking meth inside the hollow of the tree. They lit a fire to be able to see better and left it burning when they departed. That unattended fire consumed the tree. Sara even stopped to take pictures of the burning tree before she ran away. She violated her probation and has been arrested several times since 2012.

The good news about The Senator is that in 2013, artisans from across the county were given permission to make artistic items from the charred remains of the tree as a sign of respect. In 2014, a clone of The Senator was planted in the park and named The Phoenix.

Number Nine

The Gran Abuelo, a Patagonian Cypress (*Fitzroya cupressoides*) is 3,660 years old and lives in the Alerce Costero National Park in Chile. It is alive, protected, and doing well. The name, Gran Abuelo, means great-grandfather in Spanish. The tree stands sixty feet tall.

In 1933, researchers utilized a growth ring to determine the age of the tree. That means that the tree germinated and pushed through the forest floor around 1500 BCE while the Egyptians put the final touches on the pyramids, and Queen Hatshepsut was the ruler. At the same time, the Phoenicians were composing their alphabet. It was the height of the Bronze Age. A long time ago, for sure.

> The Gran Abuelo was born at the same time the Egyptians built their pyramids, 3,660 years ago.

When conquerors came to Chile, the land was cleared for settlements and the Patagonian Cypresses were cut down in record numbers because the wood is strong and good for building. As a result, the Patagonian Cypress, also known as Alerce, is an endangered species. The tree is favored because it contains a resin that slows down the time it takes to deteriorate, which explains why it was so popular as a building material.

You can visit the Gran Abuelo, but it is not an easy trip. You need a four-wheel drive, a detailed map for the roads, and a guide who knows the pathways to get into the tree's location and out again. It would not be wise to attempt this on your own.

Number Eight

Sarv-e-Abarkuh, an Abarkuh Cypress (*Cupressus sempervirens*), is a lovely name for a tree between four and five thousand years old. Legend says that it was planted by Japheth, the third son of Noah, the ark builder from the Bible. It was also said to have been planted by the Iranian Prophet Zarathushtra, Zoroaster.

If you visit the city of Abarkuh, you cannot miss the tree. It is protected by the Cultural Heritage Organization of Iran in the Yazd Province. The cedar tree has long been treasured in Persia before it became Iran in 1935. You will find the cedar tree in artwork, pottery, and elaborate garden design, which usually includes an evergreen cedar. For the cities of the desert, the green of this tree year-round is meaningful and beautiful. Cedar is regarded as a sacred tree in Zoroastrianism and Islam. Sarv-e-Abarkuh stands a hundred feet tall.

> Noah's son Japheth is said to have planted an Abarkuh Cypress that is alive today in Yazd Province, Iran.

Number Seven

The Llangernyw Yew (*Taxus baccata*) is in Conwy, Wales, United Kingdom. This tree has been gauged to be between four and five thousand years old. It is very much alive and enjoying a happy life in the churchyard of St. Digain's Church in the Llangernyw village.

This Yew holds a special place in Welsh mythology and has been associated with a spirit called Angelystor, the *Recording Angel*, who shows up once a year at Samhain (Halloween) to predict which villager will die in the coming year. A bit of a grisly job, but if spirits do truly live in trees, it is only fitting that Angelystor has a nice tree in which to dwell.

In 2002, it was celebrated as one of the Fifty Great British Trees in celebration of the Golden Jubilee of Queen Elizabeth II.

Number Six

Methuselah, a Great Basin Bristlecone Pine (*Pinus longaeva*), is 4,850 years old and lives in Inyo County in the White Mountains of California in the USA. Tom Harlan and Edmund Schulman discovered it in 1957. The biblical Methuselah lived 969 years and was the oldest living person according to the Bible. Until 2012, Methuselah the tree was considered the oldest tree in the world.

Scientific age detection revealed that the tree germinated around 2800 BCE, making it a predecessor to the pyramids and concurrent with the building of Stonehenge in the United Kingdom.

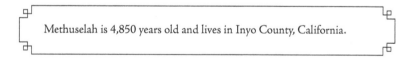

Methuselah is 4,850 years old and lives in Inyo County, California.

The tree's precise location is kept from public knowledge for fear of sabotage or desecration. However, in 2003, Jared Milarch, a tree farmer and tree conservationist, received special permission to take cuttings from Methuselah to experiment with cloning the tree. He was successful. Methuselah is now part of a nationwide nonprofit project designed to create a genetic repository for the oldest and biggest trees of every major species found in the United States.

Number Five

Prometheus, a Great Basin Bristlecone Pine (*Pinus longaeva*), lived approximately 4,900 years. It was in Wheeler Peak, Nevada. It might still be alive if it hadn't been for a student geographer in 1964, Donald Currey, who received permission to extract samples for its core, but he botched the process. According to the National Park Service, Currey discovered a tree in a grove he suspected was over four thousand years old. Local mountaineers named this tree Prometheus. It was beloved. They extended permission for him to take a core sample of the tree for exact dating.

Currey may have approached his task with improper tools, or they broke off in the tree—whatever happened resulted in the tree being cut down. A cross-section of the tree's trunk can be viewed at The Great Basin Visitor Center, but it will never replace the grandeur of the original Prometheus.

Older trees are valuable carriers of information. They have thousands of years of weather data in their rings and are invaluable for studying climate change. In 2012, an even older tree was discovered, another Bristlecone Pine in the nearby area. It has been dated at 5,065 years old.

Number Four

An **Unnamed** Great Basin Bristlecone Pine (*Pinus longaeva*) is said to be 5,075 years old. Tom Harlan dated the tree from core samples extracted by Edmund Schulman in the early 1950s. Harlan located the tree and discovered it was still living.

Then, something tragic happened. The once-in-a-lifetime core samples were lost at the Laboratory of Tree Ring Research and the Unnamed Great Basin Bristlecone Pine lost its confirmed status in 2017. Who exactly lost the samples has not been uncovered, but it is indeed an unfortunate call for the Unnamed tree.

Number Three

Old Tjikko is a Norway Spruce (*Picea abies*) located on Fulufjället Mountain in the Dalarna province in Sweden. It is carbon-dated to be 9,550 years old. Old Tjikko is a clonal tree, meaning it has regenerated new trunks, branches, and roots over millennia rather than being one individual tree of 9,500 years.

Clonal trees happen when layering occurs. As a branch meets the ground, a new root sprouts, leading to a new trunk. Old Tjikko's trunk is probably only three hundred years old, but it comes from the same tree after 9,500 years of re-rooting and regenerating.

Old Tjikko was discovered in Sweden in 2008 and thought to be the oldest tree in the world. However, it turns out, two others are ahead of her.

Number Two

The Jurupa Oak, Palmer's Oak (*Querus palmeri*), can be found in the Jurupa mountains in Crestmore Heights, California. This mighty tree is over 13,000 years old and is another clonal colony tree that has survived millennia by repeatedly cloning itself. It was discovered in 2009 with seventy clusters of stems, about 1.5 miles in width and just under four feet high.

This oak is super mighty because it shouldn't be growing where it is. It is the only Palmer's Oak in the region because the species prefers wetter, more mountainous areas. The Jurupa Mountains are arid and at a much lower altitude than these Palmers naturally enjoy.

Over the millennia, the Jurupa oak has spread out until it is now more than seventy-five feet across. Genetic testing of individual stems shows that all are part of the same organism (II 2009).

Number One

Pando, a Quaking Aspen (*Populus tremuloides*), is over 14,000 years old and the largest known aspen clone. Pando is growing in the Fishlake National Forest, Utah. Not only is it oldest tree in the world, but it may also be the oldest organism on the planet.

At first glance, Pando may look like a grove or a forest, but it is one tree sharing an underground root system of identical clones. The clonal colony was measured and encompasses 43.6 hectares (108 acres), weighing in at nearly 6,000 metric tons (6,600 short tons). It has over 40,000 stems (trunks), which die individually and are replaced by new stems growing from its roots. The root system has been tagged at 14,000 years, but it could be even older.

> Pando is the oldest tree in the world and may also be the oldest living organism on the planet.

Pando was discovered in 1976 by Jerry Kemperman and Burton Barnes and has been commemorated as one of America's Treasures. There is chat among conservationists that Pando is slowly dying. Studies have shown it is in decline and has slowed its reproduction efforts. Other reasons for the decline can be attributed to the overgrazing of young trees by local animals and the human development near to the area where Pando lives.

I have always been fascinated by the older trees. What do they know? What secrets do they keep? How many millions of people have walked by them? I love to find them wherever I go and see if they will tell me a secret. When traveling to a particular part of the globe, I like to research the oldest trees in the area and pay them a visit. Here are some trees I have had the honor of meeting.

The oldest tree in Paris, the acacia tree (*Robinia pseudoacacia* or 'Locust tree'), was planted in 1601. The oldest tree in London is the Totteridge Yew in the churchyard of St. Andrew's in Totteridge dating from 100 CE. The two-hundred-year-old Bland Oak, situated in Greater Western Sydney, New South Wales, Australia, The Ancient Yew, the Silken Thomas Tree, at St. Patrick's College estimated to be eight hundred years old, and The Hoh tree in Washington State and the clone of the original Bodhi tree in India.

There is nothing quite like standing before a magnificent tree and taking in its majesty and power. I sometimes think "If that bark could talk," what amazing things the tree would tell us. I encourage you to seek out the oldest tree in your area and spend some time with it. You'll be sure to come away with a new sense of yourself and an appreciation of what the tree has withstood through the years. Every tree on earth is our collective ancestor, and those ancestors know no distinction or separation, only pure love and acceptance for all who seek shelter from its branches, knowledge from its wisdom, and healing from its person.

In the next chapter, we will explore the sacred trees of the Celts, why they were so deeply intertwined with their lives, and what each tree did to deserve the honor.

Chapter Four

The Sacred Trees of the Celts

Trees were worshipped and cherished by the ancient Celts. It was believed that each tree had its own spirit. At the top of the list: the oak reigned supreme. It was so highly revered that many top-ranking Celts, like the bards and *filidhs*, the highest of the bard hierarchy, were said to have been buried in the hollowed-out trunk of an oak tree. I'm not sure which one had the highest honor: the tree or the Druid. The Celts considered trees to be magical, living beings. As such, they were revered, beloved, and considered sacred. Chopping one down was a civil crime, and the offender was subject to severe punishment.

According to ancient Celtic Brehon Law, there were four classes of trees, like the four classes in Celtic society. The top rung was the *airig fedo* (nobles of the wood), the *aithig fedo* (commoners of the wood), the *fodla fedo* (lower divisions of the wood), and the *losa fedo* (bushes of the wood). The group a tree was assigned to depended entirely on its economic significance (value) in terms of its fruit, timber, or size when fully grown (see Appendix A).

> In ancient Celtic Brehon Law, there were four classes of trees, like the four classes in Celtic society. The *airig fedo* (nobles), the *aithig fedo* (commoners), the *fodla fedo* (lower classes), and the *losa fedo* (lowest class).

The penalty for cutting down a tree was a fine right where it hurt the Celt the most. The seriousness of the offense was determined by the class of tree harmed and the form of damage incurred. For example, if you felled a noble wood, you had to pay by surrendering two and a half milk cows. If you cut down a common tree, it would only cost you one milk cow (Forestry Focus 2021). The Celt lost part of his ability to feed his family and make a living when he surrendered his animals.

The mighty oak was featured at Celtic seasonal celebrations like Imbolc (Candlemas), Spring Equinox (Ostara), Beltane (May Eve), Summer Solstice (Litha), Lughnasadh (Lammas), Autumn Equinox (Mabon), Samhain (Hallowe'en), and at weddings and other civil celebrations.

Celtic Wheel of Annual Holidays

The Celts revered the moon and followed its path. They named their trees and found associations between the lunar movements called Thirteen Moons and their sacred trees. They carved ritual and magic wands from the trees, each featuring a different significance and power. Each tree selected for the Celtic calendar contains magical healing properties and was used for herbal medicine, psychic protection, and the casting of spells.

Astrologically, the trees had significant meaning regarding a person's birth sign, inherent powers, natural abilities, and potential ranking in the tribe.

Celtic Tree Signs

The Celts believed that people born under a certain "tree" sign would have certain personality traits and strengths. Have a look at the trees below and find your birth month to determine what tree you resonate with, according to the day you were born. Also included are the essential oils and gemstones related to your Celtic tree sign. The Celtic year always began at Yule.

If you were born **December 24 through January 20,** your tree would be the **birch** (*Betula pendula* Roth), and you would be known as **The Achiever.**

Personality:

+ Highly driven
+ A motivator
+ Tough and reliant like the birch tree
+ Cool-headed and naturally confident (born ruler)
+ Skilled leader
+ Brighten any space with charm and quick wit

Birch: Dec. 24–Jan. 20 ✦ Birch essential oil ✦ Third chakra ✦ Black tourmaline ✦ Stag

---

Compatible Signs: Vine, Willow

Essential Oil: Birch (*Betula lenta*) extracted from the pulverized bark of the birch tree

Helps to:

+ Relieve joint and muscle pain
+ Reduce wrinkles of aging skin
+ Aids toxin removal from the body
+ Clear up skin infections due to its antifungal properties
+ Purifies the blood

Chakra: Works on the third chakra to bring back a sense of power and strength

Crystal: Black tourmaline—grounding and balancing

Animal Sign: Stag, deer—ceaseless ideas, follow through on dreams, hard worker

If you were born **January 21 through February 17**, your tree would be the **Rowan** (*Sorbus aucuparia* L.), also known as Mountain Ash, and you would be known as **The Thinker.**

Personality:

+ Visionary
+ Keen mind
+ Original, creative
+ Thought of as aloof yet burning inside with passion
+ Ability to transform
+ Highly influential in a quiet manner

> **Rowan:** Jan. 21–Feb. 17 ✦ Lavender essential oil ✦ Sixth and seventh chakras ✦ Dragon's bloodstone ✦ Cat

Compatible Signs: Ivy, Hawthorn

Essential Oil: Lavender (*Lavandula angustifolia*)

Helps to:

+ Reduce swelling and inflammation (anti-inflammatory)
+ Antibacterial—helps wounds heal
+ Increase relaxation (nervine)
+ Induce rest and sleep

Chakra: Works on the sixth and seventh chakras for psychic communication and protection

Crystal: Dragon's Bloodstone—psychic strength, endurance, and focus

Animal Sign: Cat—guardians of the underworld; resourceful, flexible, aloof, unpredictable, and mysterious

If you were born **February 18 through March 17**, your tree would be the **Ash** (*Fraxinus excelsior* L.), not related to the mountain ash, and you would be known as **The Enchanter.** Ash is related to the olive and lilac family (*Oleaceae*).

Personality:

N

- ✦ Imaginative, intuitive, naturally artistic
- ✦ Constant inner motion
- ✦ You love art, science, writing, poetry, and spirituality
- ✦ Seen as reclusive but just immersed in your own world
- ✦ Constantly self-renewing
- ✦ Unaffected by what others think about you

> **Ash:** Feb. 18–Mar. 17 ✦ Lilac essential oil ✦ Seventh chakra ✦ Chrysoprase ✦ Snake

Compatible Signs: Willow, Reed

Essential Oil: Lilac (*Syringa vulgaris*)

Helps to:

- ✦ Clear fungal infections (antifungal)
- ✦ Tighten skin—glowing complexion
- ✦ Promotes psychic awareness
- ✦ Relieves anxiety—brings harmony
- ✦ Disinfects (antibacterial)

Chakra: Works on seventh chakra to encourage clarity, vision, intention

Crystal: Chrysoprase—balance the yin and yang energy at the level of the mind and heart

Animal Sign: Snake—deep understanding, mystical wisdom, and the power to heal

If you were born **March 18 through April 14**, your tree would be the **Alder** (*Alnus glutinosa*), and you would be known as **The Trailblazer.**

Personality:

+ Charming, gregarious
+ Mingle easily with people
+ Gets along with everyone and is liked by all
+ Highly confident with a strong faith in self
+ Highly focused, dislike waste or fluff
+ Motivated by action

Alder: Mar. 18–Apr. 14 ✦ Ginger essential oil ✦ Second chakra ✦ Yellow calcite ✦ Fox

---

Compatible Signs: Hawthorn, Oak, Birch

Essential Oil: Ginger (*Zingiber officinale*)

Helps to:

+ Relieve nausea
+ Soothe arthritis pain
+ Calms digestive upset
+ Staves off colds
+ Relieves migraines

Chakra: Works on the second chakra to incite creativity and personal statement

Crystal: Yellow calcite—increases hopefulness and optimism

Animal Sign: Fox—bold personality, oozing with charm, easily accomplishes goals, and attracts followers

If you were born **April 15 through May 12**, your tree would be the **Willow** (*Salix alba* L.), and you would be known as **The Observer**.

S

Personality:

+ Highly psychic
+ Connected to the moon and mysticism
+ Keen understanding of cycles
+ Intelligent
+ Knowledgeable on many subjects
+ Acutely perceptive

Willow: Apr. 15–May 22 ⋆ Roman chamomile essential oil ⋆ Fifth chakra ⋆ Turquoise ⋆ Bull/cow

---

Compatible Signs: Birch, Ivy

Essential Oil: Roman chamomile (*Chamaemelum nobile*)

Helps to:

+ Reduce nausea and vomiting
+ Alleviate mental stress
+ Quell morning sickness
+ Aid in joint and rheumatic disorders
+ Curb pain and swelling

Chakra: Works on the fifth chakra to enhance communication and connect words with heart and intention

Crystal: Turquoise—protection, energy, serenity, positivity, happiness

Animal Sign: Bull, cow—stability, dependability, rock solid virtues

If you were born **May 13 through June 9**, your tree would be the **Hawthorn** (*Crataegus monogyna* Jacq.), and you would be known as **The Illusionist.**

Personality:

+ Excellent listener
+ Natural curiosity
+ Sense of humor
+ Sees the big picture
+ Has amazing insight
+ Gives self little credit

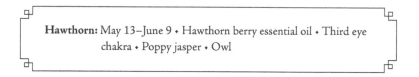

Hawthorn: May 13–June 9 ⋆ Hawthorn berry essential oil ⋆ Third eye chakra ⋆ Poppy jasper ⋆ Owl

Compatible Signs: Ash, Rowan

Essential Oil: Hawthorn berry (*Crataegus oxycanthus*)

+ Assist heart rhythm
+ Stimulate circulation
+ Lower blood pressure
+ Reduce anxiety
+ Decrease pain and inflammation

Chakra: Works on the third chakra to bring back a sense of power and strength

Crystal: Poppy jasper—deep spiritual grounding or revitalizing

Animal Sign: Owl—patience and wisdom

If you were born **June 10 through July 7**, your tree would be the **Oak** (*Quercus robur* L.), and you would be known as **The Stabilizer**.

D

Personality:

- ✦ Positive
- ✦ Confident
- ✦ All works out for the good
- ✦ Spokesperson for the underdog
- ✦ Deep respect for ancestors
- ✦ Makes a good teacher

> **Oak:** June 10–July 7 ✦ Oakmoss essential oil ✦ Second chakra ✦ Carnelian ✦ Wren

Compatible Signs: Ash, Reed, Ivy

Essential Oil: Oakmoss (*Evernia prunastri*) or bergamot (*Citrus bergamia*)

Helps to:

- ✦ Heal wounds — is antibiotic and antiseptic
- ✦ Uplift mood with orange scent and oakmoss woodsy scent
- ✦ Alleviate headaches
- ✦ Disinfect with its antiseptic and antibiotic properties
- ✦ Encourages sleep

Chakra: Works on the second chakra to foster personal power and inner emotional strength

Crystal: Carnelian—stimulates the life force energy; brings enthusiasm, power, and protection

Animal Sign: Wren—known for its complex song; emotions are expressed in melody

If you were born **July 8 through August 4**, your tree would be **Holly** (*Ilex aquifolium* L.), and you would be known as **The Ruler.**

Personality:

- ✦ Leader
- ✦ Goal-oriented
- ✦ Vigilant—seldom defeated
- ✦ Generous, kind, intelligent
- ✦ Self-confidence
- ✦ Overcome obstacles easily

> **Holly:** July 8–Aug. 4 ✦ Red thyme essential oil ✦ Third chakra ✦ Red jasper ✦ Horse

Compatible Signs: Ash, Elder

Essential Oil: Red thyme (*Thymus vulgaris*)

Helps to:

- ✦ Uplift—antidepressant
- ✦ Disinfect—antibacterial
- ✦ Bactericide
- ✦ Sedative
- ✦ Diuretic

Chakra: Third chakra for balancing the beneficent ruler

Crystal: Red jasper—grounding, insight, peace, justice

Animal Sign: Horse—royal, regal, and noble

If you were born **August 5 through September 1**, your tree would be the **Hazel** (*Corylus avellana L.*), and you would be known as **The Knower**.

Personality:

- ◆ Well informed
- ◆ Genuinely smart
- ◆ Eye for details
- ◆ Likes order
- ◆ Ability to retain information

> **Hazel:** Aug. 5–Sep. 1 ◆ Hazelnut carrier oil ◆ Fourth chakra ◆ Green jade ◆ Salmon

Compatible Signs: Hawthorn, Rowan

Essential Oil: Hazelnut carrier oil (*Corylus avellana*)

Helps to:

- ◆ Blends well with other essential oils
- ◆ Tightens skin
- ◆ Tones skin
- ◆ Regenerates cells
- ◆ Absorbs and penetrates evenly

Chakra: Works on the fourth chakra for acceptance and universal love

Crystal: Green jade—abundance, love, balance

Animal Sign: Salmon—self-preservation

If you were born **September 2 through September 29**, your tree would be **Vine** (*Vitis vinifera L.*), and you would be known as **The Equalizer.**

Personality:

+ Changeable and unpredictable
+ You can see both sides and can be indecisive
+ Loves food, wine, music, art
+ Charming, elegant, classy
+ Have the Midas touch
+ Publicly appreciated and esteemed

M

Vine: Sept. 2–Sept. 29 + Frankincense essential oil + Sixth chakra + Yellow jade + Swan

---

Compatible Signs: Willow, Hazel

Essential Oil: Frankincense (*Boswellia carteri*)

Helps to:

+ Boost mood—lift the spirits
+ Soothe wrinkles on facial skin (beauty)
+ Improves immune system
+ Reduces acne
+ Encourages comfort, peace, and calmness

Chakra: Works on the sixth chakra for intuition, inner knowingness

Crystal: Yellow jade—cheerful, energetic, helps accomplish goals

Animal Sign: Swan—style, elegance, grace, avoids drama

If you were born **September 30 through October 27,** your tree would be **Ivy** (*Hedera helix L.*), and you would be known as **The Survivor.**

G

Personality:

- ♦ Sharp intellect
- ♦ Compassionate and loyal
- ♦ Always lend a helping hand
- ♦ Silent endurance soulful grace
- ♦ Deeply spiritual
- ♦ Soft-spoken and charismatic

Ivy: Sept. 30–Oct. 27 ♦ Rose absolute essential oil ♦ Fourth chakra ♦ Rose quartz ♦ Butterfly

---

Compatible Signs: Oak, Ash

Essential Oil: Rose absolute (*Rosa x damascene*)

Helps to:

- ♦ Lighten a mood—lift the heart
- ♦ Soothe inflammation on facial skin
- ♦ Reduces feelings of nausea
- ♦ Stimulates the liver
- ♦ Gentle comfort for loss or sadness

Chakra: Works on the fourth chakra for extra love power

Crystal: Rose quartz—love, balance, forgiveness

Animal Sign: Butterfly—elegance, grace, and beauty

If you were born **October 28 through November 24,** your tree would be **Reed** (*Phragmites australis* (Cav. Trin. Ex Steudel), and you would be known as **The Inquisitor.**

Personality:

+ Deep digger into the heart of the matter
+ Discovers hidden truths
+ Keeper of secrets—honorable
+ Storyteller and story lover
+ Detective, historian, archeologist

Reed: Oct. 28–Nov. 24 ✦ Myrrh essential oil ✦ Sixth chakra ✦ Labradorite ✦ Wolf

---

Compatible Signs: Oak, Ash

Essential Oil: Myrrh (*Commiphora myrrha*)

Helps to:

+ Deeply relax via massage
+ Improve sagging skin and wrinkles
+ Relax tense situations or frustration
+ Address dandruff and strengthen hair
+ Relief for colds and coughs (inhaled)

Chakra: Works on the sixth chakra (intuition for life and others)

Crystal: Labradorite—strengthens faith in self and trust in universal powers

Animal Sign: Wolf—comfortable with the unknown, instinctual, flexible

If you were born **November 25 through December 23,** your tree would be the **Elder** (*Sambucus nigra* L.), and you would be known as **The Seeker.**

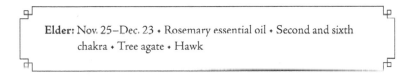

Personality:

- ♦ Deeply thoughtful—philosophical
- ♦ Extrovert and yet somewhat withdrawn
- ♦ Considerate of others
- ♦ Brutally honest
- ♦ Extremely helpful

> **Elder:** Nov. 25–Dec. 23 ♦ Rosemary essential oil ♦ Second and sixth chakra ♦ Tree agate ♦ Hawk

Compatible Signs: Alder, Holly

Essential Oil: Rosemary (*Rosmarinus officinalis*)

Helps to:

- ♦ Enhance memory
- ♦ Increase mental energy
- ♦ Soothe upset stomach
- ♦ Give relief for colds and coughs (inhaled)
- ♦ Reduce pain and inflammation

Chakra: Works on the second and sixth chakra (intuitive, instinctive sense, uncanny vision)

Crystal: Tree agate—peace and inner tranquility, immune system booster

Animal Sign: Hawk—wildly keen instinct, universal vision

These were simply how the Celts looked at their identities and traits. Many children were classified at birth for the types of lives they would lead and professions they would follow, according to the tree sign they were born under. It's neither right nor wrong, just the way it was back then. It may have been a good thing for many people and made career choices easier. We don't know. It would be hard in the modern world to be limited or exalted for your birth sign and not your achievements.

The purpose of the Celtic Tree birth sign in our day is to let the trees reveal something about us to ourselves and how our gifts are akin to a magnificent being in nature. Trees are charged with life force just as we are, and they have a lot to teach us about the macrocosm and the microcosm we call life. They teach us from the heart, from the very essence of who they are. They do not teach us through books or lectures, but from their souls.

Other trees were also sacred to the Celts. They were Alder, Apple, Ash, Birch, Blackthorn, Broom, Cedar, Elder, Elm, Fir, Furze (Gorse), Hawthorn, Hazel, Holly, Juniper, Mistletoe, Oak, Pine, Rowan, Willow, and Yew. Most of these trees will be included in the coming chapters, where we will expose our hearts and minds to fifty magnificent trees and learn what they have to give us.

We'll explore their magical qualities along with their medicinal and practical applications. By the time you finish reading about the trees, you will know a lot more about the different trees and how grateful we humans are, or should be, for the magnificent gifts the trees bring us. In the final chapters will be information as to how you can help preserve the tree kingdom. Next, we'll have a look at the sacred alphabet of secret communication created to honor trees five thousand years ago.

Chapter Five

Ogham, the Mysterious Celtic Alphabet

I have always been fascinated by Runes and Runic history. I think it's the lure of the mystery that surrounds them and that there can be only educated guesses as to how they came to be and the ways they were used. After thirty years of poking around, I have developed my theories.

My studies and curiosity about Runes introduced me to the Celtic alphabet called the Ogham. It can be pronounced as (*ow-uhm* or *oh-um*). Some historians use the spelling *Ogam*. Either one seems to be acceptable. The Ogham is the Irish equivalent of The Rosetta Stone or The Dead Sea Scrolls because it is a clue to the ancient culture that created it and what they believed.

> The Ogham is the Irish equivalent of The Rosetta Stone because it is a clue to the ancient culture that created it and what they believed.

The Ogham is an alphabet used by the Celts in 600 BCE during the Roman occupation. (Some historians date it back to the fall of The Tower of Babel in 2200 BCE.) Various scholars argue that the symbols were created from the Greek alphabet and others claim they came from Latin. The most popular answer is Latin because that's what the Romans spoke when they came to the islands.

If you aren't already familiar, the Ogham alphabet consists of twenty-five letters inscribed in wood and stone and bisected by a straight line. It was called *Beith-luis-nin*, referring to Birch, Rowan, and Ash.

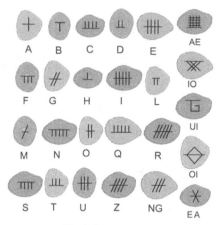

The Ogham Alphabet

The letters are divided into groups known as *aicmi* or families. The original Ogham comprises four groups of five letters for a total of twenty letters. At some later date, another group of five letters, called *forféda*, was added. These groupings reflect the counting system traditionally used in Ireland, which emphasized sets of five, twenty, and fifty. Here is the division of the groups.

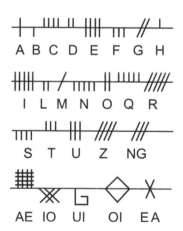

Families of Ogham Symbols

Not everyone could read the Ogham. It was an art and a practice reserved for the Bards, who were the wise men, sorcerers, musicians, astrologers, and poets. It is interesting to note that there were four levels of bards in Britain and Ireland. The *bard* was on the lowest rung, and the *filidh* was the highest. The norm was to spend three or four years at each level, called *poetry*, in the bardic schools before moving up. The fifth level was the *filidh*, and these bards were accomplished enough to be the king's official poet. When we use the word poet, we mean they could do many things that included interpreting Brehon Law, the ancient Celtic system of social government, advising about court and tribal matters, national concerns, all of which were answered in different poetic formats. These bards and *filidhs* mastered the Ogham script and could read and write it effortlessly.

A story from the tribal wars tells of one king coming up a hill to attack another king. The king under attack inscribed an Ogham on a circle of wood and tossed it in the approaching king's path. The aggressor king could not read what it said and called for his *filidh* to interpret the symbols for him. It took a few days for him to arrive. If the message was good, he needed to know that. If the message was negative, he needed to know that too before proceeding with his attack. I don't know the outcome of the incident, but for our entertainment purposes, wouldn't it be fun to assume that the invading king changed his mind and went home after waiting for so many days to find out what was written on the wood? After this incident, bards were assigned to travel with the army when it went to war.

If very few people could read and interpret the Ogham, what was it used for? Many things—creating documents, marking land, determining the boundaries of a kingdom, tombstones, memorials, and recording history for future generations.

Medieval historians associated Ogham inscriptions with secret messages, magic, and pagan lore. Interestingly, Ogham was never used for literary purposes. It was limited to short texts only. Now we know how the ancient Celts texted.

The earliest examples of Ogham letters were carved into stones. The scriptwriter began chiseling on the lower left side of the stone and worked their way up. Ogham text is read from the bottom of the left-hand edge of the stone, moving upward to the top of the stone, then across the top edge and downward to the bottom right-hand corner of the stone.

Where trees come into play is that each letter of the Ogham script was named for a tree. The Celts were emotionally and spiritually intertwined with the tree kingdom because trees were regarded as repositories of memory, lore, and the presence of spirit beings who lived within the tree. As such, trees were deemed sacred in Celtic Britain and Ireland. You couldn't have Celtic culture without trees at the center of it. This is the first reason for mentioning the Ogham in this book about magical trees. The second reason, and possibly my favorite, is that the Ogham texts are written exactly in the way a person climbs a tree: from the bottom up and continuing how they climb down the tree, along the side, and down to the right. Brilliant! Don't you love that?

At least five great trees in Ireland represent the great clans:

1. The Tree of Rossa, (*Eó Rosa*) a yew, Eó Ruis. The Yew of Rossa was said to have stood at Old Leighlin, County Carlow.

2. The Tree of Mugna (*Eó Mughna*) Eó may be the old Irish word for the yew tree, but legend has it that the Eó Mughna was a mighty oak and claimed to be the son of the original Tree of Knowledge, which resided in the Garden of Eden. According to legend, Eo Mugna's roots extend into Connia's Well, in the other world beyond the veil. Legends say it bore three fruits: apples, acorns, and hazelnuts. It stands guard over the River Shannon and the font of all wisdom. It was located at Ballaghmoon, County Kildare.

3. The Tree of Dathi (Craeb Daithí)) is known as the Muse and exercised inspiration and authority over poets, i.e., bards. It was a great ash, located at Farbill, County Westmeath.

4. The Tree of Uisnech (Craeb Uisnig) is also an ash and was the navel or center of Ireland. It was found at Uisneach, a hill that stood at the heart of what was once the High King's territory, known as Mide.

5. The Tree of Tortu (Bile Tortun), an ash, was located at Ard Breccan, near Navan, Co Meath.

In 1995, John Williams composed a symphony for Judith LeClair to honor the New York Philharmonic's 150th anniversary. It lasted twenty-six minutes and celebrated all five of Ireland's Sacred Five Trees. John Williams credited poet and author Robert Graves for his inspiration concerning the magic of the trees. The London Symphony Orchestra recorded the symphony so you could hear this amazing piece on a CD.

Each sacred tree reportedly had a permanent guard—an Irish shaman, poet, or bard, whose job was to chop down the tree hastily if foreigners invaded the land. No raider was allowed to sip the divine nature of these trees. The trees held the secrets and the magic of that province, and to capture and annihilate the tree was to have power over all the inhabitants of that land. It was only natural then that the secret alphabet, known only to a few, was carved into wood staves and chiseled into stone, fashioned to represent twenty sacred trees.

Using these symbols, the bards, *filidh*, and shamans could pass along a wealth of information to kings, subjects, and ordinary folk using these letters. Allegedly, there were even hand gestures, like sign language, that the bards used to convey messages. It is reported that they used their legs and arms as staves and marked with their hands the slashes for the letters. This was the beginning of early sign language.

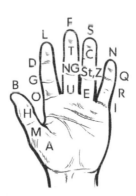

The Bard's Hand as a Mnemonic Ogham Aid

It was thought that stone carvings preceded wooden carvings or staves. But, looking at the evolution of nature, wood disintegrates over time, and it is possible, several scholars pose, that the wooden imprints decayed, leaving only the carved stones for us to investigate. Many historians agree that trees were first inscribed with the Ogham markings and then came the stones. Suffice it to say, there are conflicting positions on the full history of the Ogham. We will probably never know for sure, but we do know that the Ogham alphabet was used for communication, as a coded language, probably so the Celts could keep secrets from the Romans, and the alphabet was carved into wood, bark, leather, and stones used for sacred rituals and divination.

You can decide what you think about the Ogham alphabet. Was it patterned after the Greek alphabet?

$$A \; B \; \Gamma \; \Delta \; E \; Z \; H \; \Theta$$
$$I \; K \; \Lambda \; M \; N \; \Xi \; O \; \Pi$$
$$P \; \Sigma \; T \; \Upsilon \; \Phi \; X \; \Psi \; \Omega$$

Greek Alphabet Letters

Or the Roman?

Aa Bb Cc Dd Ee Gg
Hh Ii Jj Kk Ll Mm
Nn Oo Pp Qq Rr Ss
Tt Uu Vv Ww Xx Yy
Zz Ää Öö Üü .,?!&

Latin Alphabet Letters

Or perhaps the Phoenician?

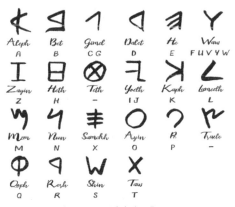

Phoenician Alphabet Letters

What alphabet do you think the Ogham alphabet resembles most?

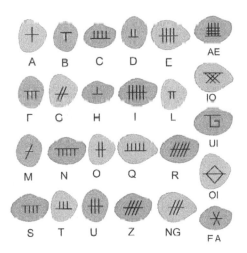

You'll be just as correct as any given scholar who has an opinion about the language the ancient Celts patterned their letters from. The most important takeaway from this alphabet is that it was made from trees and the writing pattern was designed for the way we climb a tree: upward. It is named after trees and represents their qualities. The last point about naming is the key to using the Ogham for divination and finding answers to those life issues that bring challenges and invite magic resolution.

> The most important takeaway from the Ogham alphabet is that it was made from trees; the writing pattern was designed for the way we climb up a tree; and it is named after trees and their qualities.

If you find yourself attracted to this tree-based system, you can find Ogham divination tools on Etsy, Amazon, eBay, and other sites you can search on the web. Or, best of all, you can make your own. I use a set made from hand-turned wooden acorns that have the Ogham letters burned into them. Casey "Beast" Clark in Branson, Missouri, made mine for me. I treasure them with all my heart. (His contact information is in resources at the back of the book. I receive no remuneration from him.)

I encourage you to find your way to the world of Ogham and let the trees speak their wisdom to you. After all, there's magic in every tree, and all you have to do is ask. (See the chart on this and the next few pages for divination meaning and spiritual qualities of the Ogham symbols.)

Following the chart, we will explore the magic of fifty special and magical trees.

Divination Meaning for Each Ogham Symbol

Aicme of Beith

B is for Beith	Birch	(Cleansing, hope, new beginnings)
L is for Luis	Rowan	(Protection, clear vision, psychic connection)
F is for Feàrn	Alder	(Encouragement, self-confidence, shield)
S is for Suil	Willow	(Harmony, balance, flexibility)
N is for Nuin	Ash	(Courage, strength, focus)

Aicme of Huath

H is for Huath	Hawthorn	(Heart, beauty, love)
D is for Dair/Duir	Oak	(Strength, loyalty, leadership)
T is for Teine	Holly	(Boundaries, protection, empathy)
C is for Coll	Hazel	(Wisdom, inspiration, insight)
Q is for Quert	Apple	(Wholeness, attraction, vitality)

Aicme of Muin

M is for Muin	Blackberry	(Harvest, abundance, wealth)
G is for Gort	Ivy	(Friendship, connection, support)
R is for Ruis	Elder	(Endings and beginnings, yin and yang)
Ng is for Ngetal	Reed	(Direction, purpose responsibility)
St is for Straif	Blackthorn	(Power, magical protection, positivity)

Aicme of Ailm

A is for Ailm	Elm or Fir	(Values, warrior, loyalty)
O is for Onn	Gorse	(Life force, solar power, prosperity)
U is for Ur	Heather	(Love, passion, desire)
E is for Eadha	Poplar	(Success, transformation, endurance)
I is for Idha	Yew	(Ancestral wisdom, immortality, other world connection)

Fifth Aicme

Éa for Eabhadh	Aspen	(Differences resolved)
Ór for Gold	Spindle Tree	(Community)
Ui for Uileann	Honeysuckle	(Freedom to pursue desires)
Ia for Ifín	Pine	(Make amends)
Ae for Eamhancholl	Witch Hazel	(Cleansing needed)

Other Symbols

P for Peith	Soft Birch
Eite (feather)	Marks start of texts
Spás	Space marker
Eite thuthail (reversed feather)	Marks end of texts

Chapter Six

Magical Trees A–B

Since time began, humans and animals have sought a friendship with trees. Not only did trees provide shelter from the storms and blazing sun, but they also brought comfort, nutrients, healing elements, and a sense of emotional calm and protection with them. Early peoples formed friendships with trees, and in some instances, worshipped them as deities. After all, they stood towering and tall against the sky and reached down deep within the earth, so the ancients thought, "Trees must be something special. Let's call them 'god' and bring them gifts." And thus, it began.

Of course, nothing was that simple, but it makes sense when you're toiling for food on a hot day and can lean against a shade tree for respite against the blazing sun. If you are working alone, who do you talk to? The tree, of course. Who do you tell your troubles to? Who brings you comfort without asking for anything in return? Who can you hug when your heart is breaking? Who provides you with bark for your leg or arm breaks, medicine for your ills, and tender leaves for your wounds? Ah yes, the ever-faithful tree.

As the relationship between humans and trees expanded, the trees were used to build refuges, as coverings and shelter from the rain, as warmth for cold nights, and to cook food and purify water. One thing that mattered back then was permission. Because the humans had made friends with the trees, they asked. "May I have your fronds and branches for my roof? May I please use your limbs to warm my family against the night cold? May I build my house from your trunk? May I please have some of your medicines to heal my wounds?" There was a gentle exchange between the two, and the gracious tree gave of itself to help its human friend.

That all changed when humans became greedy and thought they were entitled to all the natural resources growing before them. "I'll take this, and I'll take that," they said and began to hack away at trees, plants, and all living things. They stopped asking permission and forever changed the relationship between humans and trees, save a few wonderful souls who retained their respect and love for trees.

In that spirit, I begin this chapter by telling you all about the magnificent qualities of trees, one by one. Please take your time to get to know each one. Spend a few moments understanding them, and by the end of your reading, just as you do in life, you will find you are drawn more to some than others, and you may even call them *your* friends. I hope so. Alphabetically, then, here we go.

Magical Trees

A–B

✦ Acacia	✦ Apple	✦ Avocado	✦ Beech
✦ Alder	✦ Ash	✦ Banyan	✦ Birch
✦ Almond	✦ Aspen	✦ Baobab	✦ Boswellia

Acacia (*Acacia*)

Acacia (*Acacia*)

The acacia tree is a warm-climate loving tree that grows well under arid conditions. It has long, sturdy roots which are always searching for an underground water source. The trees grow fast but only live twenty to thirty years. The acacia is disease-resistant and is often the home to stinging ants. It grows long thorns to protect itself from predators and wildlife and creates an unpleasant flavor for all who munch on its leaves and branches.

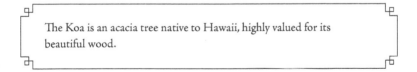

The Koa is an acacia tree native to Hawaii, highly valued for its beautiful wood.

The Koa is an acacia tree native to Hawaii, highly valued for its beautiful wood. It also grows fast, but only 10 percent of its original land coverage remains; therefore, it is an environmentally protected tree.

Acacia was the wood from which Moses built the ark of the covenant. According to Egyptian myth, the first gods were born under a cosmic acacia tree, and acacia encased the body of the deceased Osiris. Interestingly, the word *acacia* comes from the Greek *akakia*, meaning thorny Egyptian tree.

Symbolism: Divine authority, spiritual leadership, immortality, psychic connections, protection

Essential Oil: Acacia (Cassie) oil is used in bath and skincare products, folk medicine, perfumery, and massage. The flowers of the Cassie plant have antiseptic and antibacterial properties.

Gemstone: Citrine—creativity, intuition, self-esteem, confidence, abundance, counteracts negativity

Magic: The acacia tree increases psychic ability to connect with the Divine and become an authority on spiritual matters. It offers protection for spiritual pursuits. In freemasonry, it represents immortality.

Notable Associations: The Goddess Nut, Osiris, Isis, Ishtar, Diana

Medicine: Acacia is used to treat hemorrhoids and for topical treatments like wound healing and to stop bleeding. Acacia powder is used in mouth products to heal gingivitis. It is used for aiding in the control of cholesterol and has had some success with weight loss.

Caution: Some types of acacia products may contain toxins.

Practical Uses: Acacia wood is grainy, hard, and beautiful. It is in demand for flooring and furniture. It is 55 percent harder than European white oak, 23 percent harder than hickory, and 90 percent harder than carbonized bamboo, making it one of the most durable floors on the market (Acacia Wood USA 2021). In foods, acacia is used as a thickening agent due to the water-soluble gums it produces.

Conservation: Generally speaking, the acacia is not on the endangered list. It is a sustainable wood source. But in addition to the Koa trees in Hawaii, there is one variety in the British Virgin Islands that is endangered due to climate change and is now protected.

Tree Magic for Quick Stress Relief

Trees are natural givers. If there is a time when you are feeling sad, lonely, insecure, stressed, or overburdened, go outside and find a tree. Wrap your arms around it and drink in its generous magic. Breathe in its life force, vibrancy, and peace. Take a moment to visualize the energy of the earth coming in through the roots. Allow the energy to flow up through your feet and into your body.

Hold onto the tree with your arms and breathe along with the tree. Exchange energy with the tree. It will receive your sadness, loneliness, anxiety, or stress and return you to pure love, life energy, and a sense of strength and peace. Take it all in.

Turn around and connect with the tree's trunk through your spine. Absorb the strength the tree provides and breathe it in until you can feel the transference of power from the tree to you. Tune into this sacred energy exchange and relax, releasing all your cares and woes to the tree. Just as the tree intakes carbon dioxide and returns oxygen to the air, it will transmute your energies into positive qualities.

As you begin to feel better and stronger, be sure to take a moment to thank the tree for sharing its life magic with you and for imparting love from the wellspring of the earth from which it grows.

Alder *(Alnus)*

Alder *(Alnus)*

There are about thirty to thirty-five species of the alder tree. It can grow to a towering forty to eighty feet. Alder belongs to the birch family, which has light-gray bark speckled with white bits. Its leaves stay the same color when they fall.

Steeped in centuries of magic, the alder has been flourishing in swamps, streams, and rivers seemingly forever. It is associated with mystery and fairies. If your soil is bad, the alder tree will fix that problem by absorbing nitrogen from the air and distributing it back into the soil to feed other growing things.

It generously supports over seventy different types of insects, making it a haven for birds.

> Alder is associated with mystery and fairies.

Ogham: Letter F—Faern

Symbolism: Land healing, balance of masculine and feminine energy, resurrection, rebirth, protection.

The alder has both male and female catkins on its branches; therefore, it represents a balance of male and female energies and can regenerate itself.

Essential Oil: Alder oil is available from some private distillers. However, the quality and purity of private distillation and extraction cannot be guaranteed. Compatible essential oil is ginger (*Zingiber officinale*).

Gemstone: Yellow calcite—self-confidence, hope, personal motivation

Magic: Rebirth, balance, reverence, looking beneath the surface, and resurrection.

The Druids regarded the alder as the source of human life, humankind having been born from the alder. It's a fairy tree. It was believed that spirits lived in the tree, so cutting down an alder became a major because the faeries would rise up and burn your house down in revenge.

Notable Associations: Bran, Apollo, Odin, King Arthur

Medicine: Alder has been used for sore throats, diarrhea, muscle aches, nausea, fever, gum disease, shingles, rheumatism, and gout. The bark and the leaves are used to ward off fleas. The heart-shaped leaves also offer relief to skin conditions.

Caution: Alder can be toxic if not used according to a certified herbalist formulation.

Practical Uses: Alder was used in ancient times to make clogs and ship masts. Many battle shields were made from alder because of its strength. When it is felled, the alder turns from white to blood-red due to its orange sap. In building today, alder is a good substitute for birch and cherry woods. It is notably the wood used in Fender guitars.

Conservation: Alder is not endangered and is easily sustainable as a prolific wood source. However, mountain alder is currently listed as a Special Concern in Massachusetts.

Almond *(Prunus dulcis)*

Almond *(Prunus dulcis)*

The almond tree is one of the oldest nut trees cultivated by man. It is native to Iran and surrounding areas. Almonds were ground into flour and served in bread to the pharaohs. As merchants traveled the silk road, they munched on almonds to pass the time. Eventually, they brought trees to Spain and Italy to grow their own.

The almond tree grows up to thirty-five feet and features stunning pink blossoms. You need two trees to make nuts. It is the first tree to flower in spring, making it a "first" as well as the bravest due to its ability to withstand a spring frost and still bloom profusely.

Symbolism: Beauty, fertility, goddess energy, grief, hidden treasures, hope, clairvoyance

The Greeks associated the almond tree with the primeval creative force of reproduction.

Essential Oil: Almonds can be sweet or bitter, depending on the type of tree that produces them. Sweet almond is generally a carrier oil. Bitter almond contains toxic compounds.

Gemstone: Agate—enhances mental function, perception, analytical abilities, and concentration

Magic: Good luck, fertility, love relationships, abundant crops, beauty

Almond gum is used in spell work. It was said that if a young maiden sleeps beneath an almond tree and dreams of her lover, she will wake up with child.

> Keep an almond in your pocket to provide the magic for finding lost things. An almond kept in your wallet will bring you good luck and prosperity.

Notable Associations: Aaron's rod was made of the almond tree branch; the Greek friends Agdistis and Cybele, Attis, Mercury, Thoth, Hermes, Jupiter

Medicine: Almonds, high in fiber, have health benefits like lowering blood cholesterol levels. They supply protein, magnesium, calcium, Vitamin E, and potassium to the body. Almonds have been known to help regulate blood pressure and lower the odds of becoming osteoporotic.

Caution: Bitter almonds contain a poisonous compound (amygdalin) and should not be consumed.

Practical Uses: Almond wood, known as fruitwood, is used in carpentry and cabinet making. As fuel, the wood burns hot, giving off a lot of heat and leaves behind few ashes. It is a hard wood, challenging to work with, but great for tool handles, pens, spoon carvings, and walking sticks.

Conservation: Much has been written about the almond trees' water use as climate change affects drought conditions. According to research published in 2017 in the *Journal of Ecological Indicators*, for the water needed to produce them, almonds ranked among the most valuable foods grown in California for their dietary and economic benefits. Almonds support 104,000 jobs across California and contribute eleven billion dollars annually to the state's GDP. California grows close to 100 percent of commercial almonds in the US and 81 percent of almonds worldwide (Robbins 2019).

Apple *(Malus domestica)*

Apple *(Malus domestica)*

The apple tree is a member of the rose family, and it dates to 2000 BCE in Kazakhstan. The poor little apple got a bum rap because it was accused of being the fruit that brought down Adam and Eve. However, let's clear that up and tell the historical truth.

Aquila Ponticus, a second-century translator, took the liberty of translating the word mălum (meaning evil) to be an apple, using the Greek word for apple, mālum. Such a tiny distinctive mark over the letter "a." And yet, his "assumption" gave way to millennia of prejudice for the beleaguered fruit. Islamic tradition, however, commonly represents the forbidden fruit as a fig or an olive, not an apple (Adams 2006).

The apple tree figured well in Greek Mythology. The golden apple decided the ultimate prize, marriages, and even wars. The Arthurian Legends contain stories of the golden apples in Avalon, the place where wounded warriors healed. During his Twelve Labors, Hercules was dispatched to fetch the golden apples of the Hesperides.

Ogham: Letter Q—Quert

Symbolism: Winning, conquest, the ultimate prize, the top of the heap, happiness

The golden apple was a sought-after prize. The fruit of the Tree of Knowledge was, of course, the apple, and it brought down Adam and Eve's paradise because they dared to take a bite. In China, apples represent peace. They also signify wisdom, joy, fertility, rebirth, and youthfulness.

Essential Oil: There is no commercially available steam-distilled apple fruit (pulp) essential oil or apple blossom essential oil (at this time). However, fragrance oils are available that are chemically engineered to smell like green apples, red apples, or apple pie.

Gemstone: Red jasper—courage, self-confidence, emotional protection, dream recollection, sexual vibrancy

Magic: Merlin the magician was alleged to have carried a silver bough from an apple tree that hung with bells and ripened fruits. These talismans allowed him to cross into other worlds behind the veil and return to this one intact. Wands made of apple wood are said to have powers for piercing the veil into the other worlds and are only suitable for experienced magicians.

> Wands made of apple wood are said to have powers for piercing the veil into the other worlds and are best suited to experienced magicians.

Notable Associations: Venus, Avalon, Hesperides, Diana, Hercules, Hera, Idun (Norse), Snow White, William Tell, Isaac Newton, Johnny Appleseed, Morgan Le Fay

Medicine: Apple bark tea is a tonic and can relieve gas, fever, helps with digestion, and can neutralize the effects of fatty foods.

Caution: Apple seeds contain amygdalin, which, when digested, releases the toxic chemical cyanide. Eat the apples, not the seeds, for safety.

Practical Uses: Fine furniture, tool handles, and small specialty items. Apple wood shrinks; therefore, it may change over time. It needs to be fully dried before burning for heat.

Conservation: Apple trees are not endangered, but there is a hearty movement by conservationists to manage abandoned apple orchards and farms and bring them back to fruition.

Ash *(Fraxinus)*

Ash *(Fraxinus)*

There are sixty-five species of the ash tree in the world. The most commonly found ash tree throughout the UK and most of Europe is known scientifically as *Fraxinus Excelsior*.

The tree forms a canopy dome where two or more are gathered. Ashes like a warm, cool climate and can grow 30 to 120 feet tall. They produce miniature purple flowers arranged in clusters pollinated by the wind. Ash is a smokeless burning wood, giving off only medium heat.

Ogham: Letter N—Nuin

Symbolism: Strength, power, divine connection, authority, protection

The ancient Irish believed the ash tree (also known as the Rowan tree) had healing qualities and saw it as one of the trilogies of sacred trees, along with the oak and the hawthorn.

Essential Oil: Ash oil is available from some private distillers. However, the quality and purity of private distillation and extraction cannot be guaranteed. Lilac *(Syringa vulgaris)* essential oil is compatible.

Gemstone: Chrysoprase—equalizes emotional balance, heals a broken heart, relaxes, and helps prevent nightmares

Magic: Divination, prophecy, and inspiration

Ash wood was used by Druid priests to make wands. It is the bridge between heaven and earth. Ash is used in advanced magic. Ash is the wood of the scholar, poet, and writer. Odin chose this tree to hang upside down for nine nights to receive enlightenment. It is from this tree he created the first human. Ash promotes spiritual love and health. Faeries love ash and are comfortable being in the presence of this tree. A staff made of it is said to possess the power and authority of The World Tree. Odin's spear was carved from ash wood. Place ash leaves under your pillow to foster prophetic dreams.

> Ash wood was used by Druid priests to make wands. It is the bridge between heaven and earth. Odin chose this tree to hang upside down for nine nights to receive enlightenment.

Notable Associations: Odin, Poseidon, Lir, Loki, Nemesis, Uranus, Thor, Mars

Medicine: Ash tree bark is said to be edible because it has anti-inflammatory properties as well as antirheumatic abilities to soothe arthritis and rheumatism. It is said to help with the pain and swelling of gout and reduce bladder problems. White ash bark treats dysmenorrhea. Chewing gum produced from the tree contains mannitol. Ash wine is made as a curative for arthritis, and the leaves are useful for snake bites.

Caution: Not all ash trees (species) are created with equal medicinal properties. Be careful when ingesting, especially during pregnancy.

Practical Uses: Ash is a hard wood and is used to make things that require durable strength, like baseball bats, tool handles, and wooden bows. It is frequently used for making electric guitars but not usually for acoustic ones. It is a strong, hard, and flexible wood.

Conservation: Unfortunately, ash trees are often targeted by the Emerald Ash Borer (type of beetle), now active in thirty-five states and five Canadian provinces. They destroy the vascular system of the plant and induce the quick death of the tree. The black ash tree is on the verge of extinction due to an infestation of the invasive species. This nasty little bug has managed to kill off 7.5 billion ash trees already, and there will likely be no more after the decade is over (Home Stratosphere 2021).

Conservators are attempting to create a genetically diverse, resistant seedling suitable for replanting the diseased ash trees. In the UK, the ash is threatened by *ash dieback*, a disease caused by the *Hymenoscyphus fraxineus* fungus.

Whittling Tree Magic—How to Make Your Wand

You will need:

- A utility knife or a sharp pocketknife
- Eye protection
- Hand protection
- One piece each of sandpaper grit: 150, 320, and 600
- Dust mask
- Small hand saw
- Stain, paint, or natural juice from the tree: berries, seeds, or fruit

Directions

1. Find a branch from a tree you like. One that has fallen is best, or you can ask permission of the tree before helping yourself to a branch that is still attached. Cut it off with a sharp blade. Seal the tree wound with tea.

2. Cut it to the size you want and peel away the bark.

3. Determine if you like the shape or begin carving your shape, design, Runes, Ogham, or symbols you like. (Wear protective gear.)

4. Once you have the design you want, sand the wand until smooth.

5. If the wood is young, you may want to allow it to dry and age before staining or painting.

---

6. Paint or stain your wand. Let it dry. Perhaps you want to spray it with a clear sealing coat to protect it.

7. Add stones, feathers, leather trim, twine, or anything natural you choose to your wand.

8. Apply a few drops of essential oil (diluted) to the wand to add natural vibration energy.

9. Name your wand and designate it to sacred work and white light.

The wand will carry the energies and qualities of the tree from which it was formed. Those energies will be available to you twenty-four seven.

Aspen (*Populus tremuloides*)

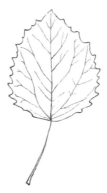

Aspen (*Populus tremuloides*)

Aspen is native to cooler areas of North America. Several species are referred to by the common name aspen. It has many names: quaking aspen, trembling aspen, American aspen, mountain or golden aspen, trembling poplar, white poplar, and popple, as well as others. The aspen is mesmerizing to the eye because it displays immaculate bark and golden leaves during the autumn. Some say it quakes because it is ashamed that it was the wood used for the cross of Jesus. This is pure nonsense. If the true cross had ever been found, it was most likely made from oak, cypress, sycamore, or cedar—the trees flourishing in the area at that time. The aspen grows quickly but does not live long—a maximum of twenty-five years.

Symbolism: Communication with the next world, protection from spiritual harm

The aspen respects ancestry and opens communication between the people on Earth and those who have passed. Different cultures and belief systems associate the wind with the voice of the Spirit. The boughs are believed to contain the voice of the wind, available for anyone to hear who will stop to listen. The aspen, therefore, encourages contemplation and meditation.

Essential Oil: Aspen oil is available from some private distillers. However, the quality and purity of private distillation and extraction cannot be guaranteed. Melissa (*Melissa officinalis L.*) essential oil is compatible.

Gemstone: Golden topaz—divine light, ancient wisdom, understanding, connection to ancestors

Magic: Protection, eloquence, anti-theft, peace.

The tree wood holds powers of protection from spiritual harm and spells. An aspen leaf is placed under the tongue and makes the bearer more eloquent, traditionally considered a gift of the Faerie Queen. Aspen is used to protect your goods against thievery. The tree brings a message of peace.

> An aspen leaf is placed under the tongue and makes the bearer more eloquent, traditionally considered a gift of the Faerie Queen.

Notable Associations: Persephone, Hades, Oya

Medicine: Aspen bark has been used for rheumatoid arthritis (RA), nerve pain, and pain caused by pressure on the sciatic nerve (sciatica) due to its anti-inflammatory, astringent, and antiseptic actions.

Caution: Pregnant or lactating women should not use aspen medicine.

Practical Uses: Aspen was used for making shields because it carried the magical qualities of protection. It is a light wood and buoyant and was used for oars, paddles, splints, and even flooring because it does not burn well.

Conservation: In 1991, a huge conservation effort began in Scotland. Aspen has probably suffered the most from deforestation. It rarely produces seeds, and when it does, red deer eat the young shoots. Colonies are being fostered away from predators because the aspen tree is the home to many endangered bugs and lichen. In the western USA, there is a movement to study *aspen decline*. The trees are being researched for diseases, insects, and other geographical reasons for the decline.

Avocado *(Persea)*

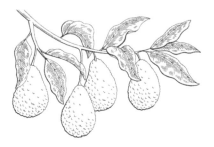

Avocado *(Persea)*

The avocado tree was a sacred tree for the Egyptians, and they fashioned magical wands from the wood. Wood cuttings were used in their sacrificial fires. The tree can grow fifty to sixty feet high.

There are approximately twenty cultivars of this tree spread throughout the world. However, this tree should not be confused with *Persea americana*, cultivated and grown in Mexico. The Egyptian *Persea* was regarded in such sacred esteem that Emperor Arcadius forbade the uprooting or sale of any *persea* tree in Egypt. *Persea Mimusops* was found in temples, tombs, and the pyramids of the ancients.

In Mesoamerica, archeologists date the avocado tree back to 5000 BCE—although it may be older than that. During the Spanish Christianization of South America, this aphrodisiac fruit was used by the Incas in Peru and is represented on the Mayan calendar. Of course, the conquerors took the trees back to Spain where they adopted the name of *Spanish Fruit* in Europe. The Aztec name for avocado was *ahuacatl*, meaning testicle.

Symbolism: Rebirth, lust, beauty, wealth, and love

Essential Oil: Some may refer to avocado oil as an essential oil, but that's not entirely accurate. Viscous and green-colored, avocado oil is considered a carrier oil.

Gemstone: Green jade—protection from harm, promotes harmony, brings good luck and friendship

Magic: Planting an avocado tree in your yard is believed to bring love into the home. Seduce your lover with foods made from avocado, for a radiant face, use half an avocado with a quarter cup honey, combine, and apply to your face. Wait one hour before removing the masque. Boiling the pits of avocados creates a lovely, natural pink dye. Dry avocado pits for two weeks, then add them to spell bags for abundance, luck, and attracting magic.

Notable Associations: Perseus, Bastet, Osiris

Medicine: The oil from the fruit is good both as a medicine and for cooking. Avocado is said to reduce high cholesterol, calm psoriasis, and arthritis outbreaks, increase sexual desire, halt obesity, help hair growth, and improve heart health.

Caution: Priestesses of Apollo chewed the leaves and inhaled their smoke to induce a psychic state of mind; however, this is not recommended due to toxicity and heart and liver damage. Before using avocado oil, be sure to check for allergies.

Practical Uses: Avocado is a soft hardwood, stable, easy to work with, and has an elegant, streaky color and knotty grain. Its oily texture is excellent for carving and sculpting. The fruit has culinary and health supporting attributes when consumed.

Conservation: It is currently not an endangered species. It is grown for its oils and fruit. Mexico produces the most avocados globally, with the Dominican Republic coming close behind.

Avocado Tree Magic—Spell for Love

You will need

+ Two avocados

+ Two colors of ribbon (each twenty inches): one representing you and one representing your intended

+ Two pieces of red ribbon: one twenty inches and the other twelve inches

Directions

1. If possible, feed your intended something you have made from the meat of the avocado fruit. Keep two seeds for magical use.

2. Peel the outer layer from the seeds.

3. Braid the three colors together until you have a multicolored lanyard.

4. Hold the seeds in your hand and wrap the braided ribbon around the seeds.

5. Tie off the end underneath and unravel the leftover to form a bow or a knot.

6. Thread the twelve-inch red ribbon through the twist of the lanyard to form a loop to hang your creation.

7. While holding the wrapped seed in your hands, say:

> *Wherever you go, I go.*
> *Wherever I go, you go.*
> *Our love is true, that I know.*
> *Together, we shall always go.*

8. Continue: Visualize your intended, visualize yourself. Picture you both happy and sharing your love. Speak the words: *"This union is blessed; it is mutual and forever. Blessed be."[1]*

9. Hang your avocado seed package someplace safe and where both of you will share the energy.

10. As you walk by it, praise it and thank it for the work it is doing.

Banyan *(Ficus benghalensis)*

Banyan *(Ficus benghalensis)*

The Banyan tree is native to places like Pakistan, Nepal, India, Sri Lanka, China, Taiwan, Central America, South America, and a few tropical places in the United States. The genus refers to the Latin name for fig, and the species comes from the city of Bengal in India. It got its name from the traders called banians who made their trade deals under the shade of the Banyan tree.

One of the unique qualities of this tree is that it has aerial roots which grow in shallow and swampy soils. To support the enormous trunk, the roots span a larger surface area. The leaves are so large, thick, and leather-like that many indigenous peoples use the leaves as plates and for shelter.

In Hindu mythology, the Banyan tree is called *Kalpavriksha*, which means the tree fulfills the wishes of the devotees and provides material gains for them.

---

1 Note: When you close your ritual or blessing, you may use the words that are most comfortable to you: *and so it is; so mote it be; amen; blessed be; abracadabra,* which means I create as I speak, or any combination of words that are familiar and meaningful to you.

Banyan leaves are so large, thick, and leather-like that many indigenous peoples use the leaves as plates and shelter.

Symbolism: Immortality and longevity.

It can live for two hundred years. The Banyan tree is associated with Yama, the God of death, represents one's spiritual aspirations, and is equivalent to the hermit archetype.

Essential Oil: Banyan oil is available from some private distillers. However, the quality and purity of private distillation and extraction cannot be guaranteed.

Compatible essential oil: Neroli (*Citrus aurantium L.*); lifts depression, alleviates anxiety, restores emotional balance.

Gemstone: Aventurine—prosperity, longevity, leadership, compassion, and perseverance

Magic: The Banyan tree fulfills wishes, provided you make them earnestly and with a purity of heart.

Notable Associations: Yama, Lord Vishnu

Medicine: The Banyan tree's sap, like latex, can be applied externally over the joints. Pain has been known to disappear after a few applications. It is used in Ayurveda for many ailments. The parts of the Banyan tree used are aerial root, latex, fruits, buds, and leaves. It has antifungal and antibacterial qualities and treats diarrhea, tooth and gum disease, boosts immunity, lifts depression, and can lower cholesterol.

It contains B Sitoster, esters, glycosides, leucocyanidin, quercetin, sterols, and friedelin. It is also rich in ketones, polysaccharides, sitosterol, and toglic acid (Librate.com Banyan Tree Benefits 2010).

Caution: There are no known adverse effects from using the products of the Banyan tree. Although not recorded, caution is advised against using Banyan tree medicine if pregnant or breastfeeding.

Practical Uses: The sap of the lac insect, a parasite to the tree, is used to make shellac. Paper is made from the wood. In India and Pakistan, twigs are collected and sold as toothpicks.

Conservation: The Banyan tree is being cut down to build and expand. It is a sacred tree to the culture and represents Lord Shiva. Conservation is needed—now.

Baobab *(Adansonia)*

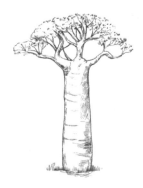

Baobab *(Adansonia)*

The baobab trees have unusual barrel-like trunks and are long-lived. Because they look somewhat odd, legend says that the devil plucked the baobab out of the ground and stuck it headfirst back into the ground, leaving its roots dangling in the air.

Even though odd-looking, the baobab tree is called the Tree of Life. It can provide shelter, clothing, food for animals and humans in the savannah regions of Africa. There are eight different species of the baobab tree. The baobab tree can live up to three thousand years and grows quite huge, reaching heights from sixteen to ninety-eight feet and has trunk diameters of twenty-three to thirty-six feet.

Spirits are said to live within the tree, and damaging one can harm the spirits.

The Baobab tree is called the *Tree of Life* in Africa.

Symbolism: Ancient awareness, divine communication, blessings, earth wisdom, knowledge, spiritual power, sustenance

Essential Oil: Baobab seed oil is cold-pressed from seeds for various uses, from cooking and hair care to skincare. It is rich in omega-3 fatty acids.

Gemstone: Smoky topaz—reduces fear, promotes positivity, relieves stress and anxiety

Magic: It is said that gazing at a baobab tree evokes ancient feelings and spirits. It is believed that if you cut down a baobab tree, you will be punished by death. The same is true for collecting twigs or branches, even those that have fallen on the ground. You will never have a wand of the baobab tree but contemplating its very image should be enough to evoke magic.

To gaze at a Baobab tree is to evoke ancient feelings and spirits.

Notable Associations: Osanyin, Aja, Oko, Ososhi

Medicine: Baobab fruit is used for malnutrition, asthma, and to repel mosquitos. The fruit and leaves contain many nutrients that promote immune support and gut health. The fruit dries on the tree and produces a 100 percent superfood. It helps balance the body's pH and defends against chronic diseases and conditions like hypertension, arthritis, and vitamin-D deficiency.

Caution: There is not enough scientific information to know how baobab might work for any medical condition—however, the fruit and leaves contain many nutrients.

Practical Uses: Fiber from the bark is used for rope and cloth in many places, and the trees supply raw materials for hunting and fishing tools. Naturally hollow or excavated trunks can serve as water reserves or temporary shelters. Some have been used as prisons, burial sites, and stables for animals. The fruit of the baobab tree is called monkey fruit, which can be ground into powder and be used for rituals, food products, and worship of the gods.

Conservation: The baobab tree has been facing a flowering challenge, the lack of which has led to massive death in Ethiopia. Conservation and rehabilitation measures are necessary to save the baobab trees from disappearing. Baobabs are critically threatened by land-use changes and unsustainable harvesting due to growing demands for Non-Timber Forest Products (NTFP), generally defined as products derived from biological resources. That would include mushrooms, berries, bark, burls, conks, cones, boughs, diamond willow, landscaping transplants, and sap.

Tree Spell for Courage, Peace, Prosperity

If you are seeking courage, strength, peace of mind, prosperity, healing, romance, forgiveness, or career moves, you can ask the tree for help to attract the things you want.

You will need:

+ A small empty bottle or jar or vial
+ Ribbon or string
+ A candle
+ Quartz crystal or stone compatible with the tree
+ And, where applicable, essential oil made from the tree, bark, seeds, needles, roots

Directions

1. Ask permission of the tree to utilize some branches, leaves, dirt and twigs, berries, or seeds from it.
2. Gather: small twigs, leaves, seeds, berries, fruit, dirt, or sand from around the tree (do not expose roots). Place 1 tablespoon of the items in the container (or scale down if container is smaller), creating layers of each of the items: dirt or sand, crushed leaves, twigs, or seeds.
3. Add: a stone (or stones) or crystal compatible with the tree.
4. Add: 3 drops of the essential oil made from the tree.

---

5. Add: handwritten piece of paper with your request. State your request in the present tense with affirmative words. Choose one from among these samples: I am enjoying the love and companionship I deserve. I have everything I need and rest in the secure feeling it brings me. I am forgiven, I forgive, and life abounds with joy. I am happy; I am loved. My mind and soul are at peace, and I am relaxed. My job fills me with feelings of success and fulfillment. My mind, body, and soul are healed and restored according to my beliefs. My life is whole, perfect, and complete.

6. Add: personal item representing you: a stone, medallion, initial, piece of jewelry, or ring you have worn.

7. Replace the lid or cork on the container. Tie with ribbon or string. Add an amulet, charm, icon, or symbol, or use a small twig from the tree or a nut.

8. Light the candle and drip wax over the lid to seal it to the bottle. Allow the candle wax to drip over the bottle and down the sides. Use as many candles as colors you choose to drip.

9. Place the bottle on your altar or in a place where you will see it to remind you of what you have attracted to yourself using tree magic.

10. Step aside, accept the results, and let the tree works its magic for you.

Beech *(Fagus)*

Beech *(Fagus)*

Beech trees are ancient, ranging from 225 years upward. Some have ancient characteristics that date from around 175 years. There are three types of beech:

notable, veteran, and ancient. A veteran beech can be 125 to 200 years of age, and a notable beech may be 75 to 150 years old (Woodland Trust 2021). Beech trees are favorites for courtyards and lining streets. The most famous grove may be the dark hedges in Northern Ireland featured in *Game of Thrones*.

The beech is called the *Queen Mother of the Woods*, sharing her title with the kingly oak, who is *King of the Woods*.

Symbolism: Protection of the heart, trust, new growth, unlocking wisdom, nurturing, letting go of old ways, knowledge.

Essential Oil: Beech nut oil is available from some private distillers. However, the quality and purity of private distillation and extraction cannot be guaranteed.

Compatible essential oil: Lavender (*Lavandula angustifolia*) provides antibacterial, antiviral, antimicrobial, anti-inflammatory, and nervine properties.

Gemstone: Silver jasper—strength, stability, grounding

Magic: Wishes or prayers uttered under a beech go straight to heaven. Carry slivers of beech for protection and to welcome ancient knowledge into your heart. Use guidance from the past to make decisions about the future.

Notable associations: Zeus, Diana, Nerthus, Loki

Medicine: The leaves of beech trees have antibacterial properties, and Native Americans traditionally used them for treating tuberculosis. The antibacterial leaves can also be used as a poultice for burns. Astringent beech bark was a traditional remedy for minor ailments like boils, piles, and skin ailments.

Caution: Do not use while pregnant or breastfeeding. Excessive consumption of the nuts may cause poisoning.

Practical Uses: Beech wood makes furniture, bowls, baskets, and kitchen utensils. Tar from the timber can be used to make creosote.

Conservation: In Ohio, there is beech leaf disease taking a toll on trees. No one knows how far this will progress, but, for now, beech trees are not endangered.

Birch (*Betula*)

Birch (*Betula*)

The birch tree (*Betula*) comes in many colors. There is a black birch, yellow birch, paper birch, gray birch, red birch (also known as water birch), all named for the color of their bark. They have small leaves and cylindrical cones, called samara, with over one million seeds, as fruit. The bark is thin, which sets them apart from other trees. Commonly used for ornamental purposes, these trees are tall and elegant with distinctive markings. It is normally a short-lived, fast-growing, and flexible tree. However, birch trees can live from thirty to two hundred years, depending on climate and soil conditions.

Ogham: Letter B—Beith

Symbolism: Renewal, protection, new beginnings, blessings

Birch is known as the *White Lady of the Woods*. She stands tall, elegant, strong, and beautiful. She is the first to show signs of life in the spring and hails as the first tree to grow after the ice age. Birch grows everywhere in the north, except the coldest places. "Birch has the fresh innocence of the Maiden, the generosity of the Mother, and the silent courage of the Crone" (Gruben 2017). Her time of year is between Yule and Imbolc, in the winter.

It is recorded that the white tree bark illuminates the darkness in the deep night forest. Birch trees were used as ancient ladders up into the sky for seekers to reach the cosmic world of spirits and gods. It was suggested that these ascensions took place during trance. Birch tree groves provided psychic protection from invading or unwanted spirits and magical spells.

> Birch has the fresh innocence of the Maiden, the generosity of the
> Mother, and the silent courage of the Crone.

Essential Oil: Several components make up the birch essential oil: salicylic acid, methyl salicylates, betulene, and betulenol. Birch oil has a fresh, minty aroma, a sharp and familiar fragrance that is soothing and calming.

Gemstone: Black tourmaline—absorbs negativity, grounding, healing

Magic: Inception, fertility, and renewal

Birch paper is excellent for spells. Birch trees were used as maypoles and fuel for the sacred fires at Yule, Imbolc, Beltane, Lughnasa, and Samhain. Burning a birch yule log was said to bring good luck for the coming year.

Notable Associations: Freya, Venus, Brighid, Thor

Medicine: Birch is a natural diuretic, and it has been used as a tea to cleanse and detoxify the urinary system. Externally, it can be applied for use as a skin tonic, tightening sagging skin, and as a remedy for sore and aching muscles. Birch has been used to remedy arthritis, rheumatism, and bone health. Birch is anti-inflammatory, antiseptic, anti-rheumatic, and astringent. Native Americans used birch paste for traditional wound healing. Birch contains *betulin* and *betulinic* acid used in the pharmaceutical industry.

Caution: The birch tree contains methyl salicylate, the active ingredient in aspirin. Essential oils are made from the bark. It should not be used with blood-thinning medications, by the elderly, or by people with bleeding disorders.

Practical Uses: In the olden days, birch's flavor, wintergreen, was used in chewing gums. Birch tree sap is still used as a winter food source for some indigenous peoples of Siberia and North America. Birch sap is used to manufacture wine and beer in northern Europe, Russia, and China. It can also serve as a substitute for sugar. Birch syrup, made of birch sap, is used as a dressing for pancakes (Soft Schools 2020).

In the olden days, birch's flavor, wintergreen, was used in chewing gums.

Conservation: Out of sixty birch species, eleven are listed as endangered mainly due to habitat destruction and various fungal diseases (Soft Schools 2020).

Boswellia *(Boswellia serrata) and (Boswellia sacra)*

Boswellia (*Boswellia serrata*)

This species is also called the frankincense or olibanum tree. The sap from the tree is the most popular and widely used resin in history for rituals of purification, protection, consecration, and healing. History places it as having been around since 1500 BCE, but most like a few thousand years before that, unrecorded.

The *Boswellia sacra* tree is a smaller species and grows to a height of six to twenty-six feet. It produces sap when it is eight to ten years old. You might see a *Boswellia sacra* tree growing in a crevice, along a mountain slope, or in places where a tree does not usually grow. It thrives in the dry, mountainous, and hilly regions of India, Africa, and the Middle East.

The bark is paper-thin and must be carefully extracted from the tree. Legend tells us that when the Phoenix arose from the ashes, she made her nest in the Boswellia tree.

Symbolism: Protection, healing, consecration, purification

Essential Oil: Frankincense, also known as olibanum, is made from the resin of the Boswellia tree. This tree typically grows in the dry, mountainous regions of India, Africa, and the Middle East.

Gemstone: Tiger's Eye—helps to release fear, anxiety, and aids in restoring harmony and balance

Magic: You can carry a piece of frankincense resin as protection. Place a small bowl of the resin as an offering to the deities you prefer. It is a wonderful essential oil for use in anointing or consecration. Burned, it produces a magical aroma and creates a feeling of the sacred when the scent is inhaled.

> Carry a piece of frankincense resin as protection. Place a small bowl of the resin as an offering to the deities you prefer. Frankincense essential oil is used in anointing or consecration.

Notable Associations: Ra, Apollonius, Hephaestus, Venus, Sol, Buddha, Brahma, Vishnu, Shiva

Medicine: Frankincense is good for helping to reduce stress and to encourage emotional healing. Frankincense can be burned to create an aroma, used as an oil in a diffuser, added to cosmetics to help attend to wrinkles, used as an acne healer, and is a perfect healer for sensitive skin. Used as a hydrosol, it can soothe facial and body skin and moisturize it. The analgesic properties of frankincense can help relieve pain, headaches, and general muscle tension. Frankincense can also help with respiratory ailments and clear up congestion and mucous.

Caution: Do not use frankincense if you are pregnant or breastfeeding or around children under two.

Practical Uses: *Boswellia sacra* and *Boswellia serrata* are both excellent sources of pulp for the manufacture of high-quality paper.

Conservation: Despite its long history as a sacred plant, *Boswellia* trees today are looking at a grim future. According to a study published in the *Journal of*

Applied Ecology, the trees are threatened by various pressures that may reduce their numbers by 90 percent in the next few decades. Young saplings are not surviving; trees are seeding less frequently and with decreased viability. Over-harvesting is a factor, but so are predators and increased fires (Frankincense and the Magi's Endangered Tree 2011).

The other piece is that so many people are harvesting the sap from the trees that they have deep cuts and are open doors for insects. Scientists and conservationists are experimenting with new, less invasive methods to harvest the sap without destroying the healthy tree. Only buy resin that you know has been sustainably harvested.

Chapter Seven

Magical Trees C–F

Magical Trees

C–F

✦ Cedar	✦ Cottonwood	✦ Eucalyptus
✦ Cherry	✦ Cypress	✦ Fig
✦ Chestnut	✦ Dogwood	✦ Fir
✦ Coconut	✦ Elder	
✦ Coffee	✦ Elm	

Cedar (*Cedrus*)

Cedar (*Cedrus*)

The cedar tree (*Cedrus*) is native to the Mediterranean and western Himalayan mountains. It is found at altitudes of 3,200 to 7,000 feet in the Mediterranean region and 5,000 to 10,500 feet in the Himalayas. King Solomon chose the cedar tree for the construction of his temple. The Phoenicians built ships from them, and the resin from the trees was used extensively in the Egyptian mummification process. At one time, the cedars of

Lebanon *Cedrus libani* were destroyed by overuse, but thanks to reforestation, they are growing anew but now face climate change as their biggest enemy. Some of the trees are over three thousand years old.

Symbolism: Strength, longevity, eternity, gateway to higher realms, prosperity.

Essential Oil: Cedarwood (*Cedrus*) essential oil is a substance derived from the cedar trees' needles, leaves, bark, and berries. There is a large selection of varieties of cedar trees found around the world. Some trees referred to as cedars are juniper trees.

Gemstone: Bronzite—courage, unsettled emotions, power to move forward, protection

Magic: Fashioned as doors to sacred spaces, cedar is used for healing, purification, promoting peaceful thoughts, and surfacing messages from the inner sage. Designate sacred spaces around the perimeter using cedar chips or shavings. Use a cedar wand to bless and create a holy place. Use cedar in sweat lodge ceremonies. Cedar medicine wards off external forces.

Notable Associations: King Solomon, Gilgamesh, Jesus, Artemis, Athena, Rhiannon

Medicine: The essential oils extracted from cedar leaves or cut wood release oils that repel insects, molds, fungi, bacteria, and some viruses.

Caution: Test for allergies. Always properly dilute your cedar oil; never ingest.

Practical Uses: Cedar trees are grown for their durable, rot-resistant, highly scented wood, which comes from resinous oils within its structure. Cedar wood is resistant to harsh weather and is used for shingles, shakes, and fences. Items made from cedar can last for a long time. Cedar oil is a repellant of insects, like moths, so it is used for lining in closets to save wool from hungry moths.

Conservation: There is a debate between wildlife and grazing land proponents regarding cedar trees. Cedar is a prized wood, but it expands and takes over grasslands, creating a fire hazard. It has also been reported that one cedar tree can use up to thirty gallons of water a day. The American burying beetle is being pushed out of its lands by the cedar trees. The beetle is crucial to ecosystems in the area. The Clanwilliam cedar is endangered in South Africa. Alaska's ancient yellow cedars are suffering a double whammy from the climate crisis and logging in the Tongass National Forest. Hopefully, they will get some help, or they will be gone by 2070.

Cedar Tree Magic—Purification Ritual

You will need

+ Cedar essential oil

+ A piece of paper, about six by six inches

+ Pen or pencil

+ A pedestal glass or chalice

+ Cedar chip incense

Directions

1. Write on your paper what you want to cleanse and purify.

2. Begin folding the paper until you end up with a one-inch square.

3. Place the folded paper in the glass and add 5 drops of essential oil to purify. Say while adding the oil:

    I ask that this cleansing oil and the spirits of purification hereby cleanse what was before and transform the tainted energy into purity and fresh light. From this point forward, black becomes white, the contaminated morphs to clear and clean. All is forgiven and reborn. I am free.

(Note: When you close your ritual or prayer, you may use the words that are most comfortable to you: *And so it is; so mote it be; amen; blessed be; abracadabra,* which means I create as I speak, or any combination of words that are familiar and meaningful to you.)

4. To celebrate the purification and transformation, light the cedar incense and say:

    Today begins anew. The slate is clear; the page is blank. I will write my new intentions and create my new life from this moment forward. I ask all my guides and guardians to support this cleansing and purification and guide me into a new beginning. (Close prayer.)

---

5. Take a moment to gently inhale the aroma of the cedar smoke. Allow it to fill you and feel the clarity and newness it brings.

Cherry *(Cerasus)*

Cherry *(Cerasus)*

The cherry blossom, considered sacred to the Japanese emperor, is the national flower of Japan. The mayor of Tokyo, Yukio Ozaki, gifted the USA with three thousand cherry trees in 1912. They were planted in Washington, DC. In a reciprocal gesture, the United States gifted Japan with flowering dogwoods in 1915.

The mayor of Tokyo, Yukio Ozaki, gifted the USA with three thousand cherry trees in 1912. They were planted in Washington, DC. In a reciprocal gesture, the United States gifted Japan with flowering dogwoods in 1915.

The cherry tree is the first to blossom in the spring, heralding new beginnings and rebirth from the winter snows. Cherries are in the same genus as peaches, plums, apricots, and almonds. These plants are cousins to apples, pears, and hawthorns. All the above are members of the enormous rose family of plants. Their family resemblance is shown clearly in the blossoms of all these species, which resemble small, wild roses.

The fruit is a stone fruit generally heart-shaped, about two cm. (one inch) in diameter, and varies in color from yellow to red to nearly black.

Symbolism: New awakenings, rebirth, good fortune, love, and romance A cherry tree also represents survival, fertility, stability, and focus.

Essential Oil: Cherry essential oil has a rich, ripe, fruity aroma, warmth, and happiness. It is used in aromatherapy for skincare, haircare, massage, bathing, making perfumes, soaps, scented candles, and more.

Gemstones: Ruby—passion, vitality, opens the heart, stirs Tantric energy Rose quartz—unconditional love, relationship healing

Magic: Love spells excel with cherry wood, incense, oils. Use the focused, earthy energy for working with animals. Cherry wood wands are centered and grounded with earth energy.

Notable Associations: Kraneia the dryad nymph

Medicine: Cherry has anti-inflammatory properties, so it can be used for colds, coughs, and bronchitis. It has also been used for diarrhea, gout, and digestive disorders. Some claim it helps induce sleep because it is a sedative. The potent components in tart cherries have been demonstrated to deliver high-level protection against inflammatory and degenerative diseases, including cardiovascular disease, metabolic syndrome, and neurodegenerative diseases such as Alzheimer's (Life Extension 2021).

Caution: Consuming large amounts of cherry juice may lead to indigestion and diarrhea and could cause an allergic reaction if one is allergic to cherry fruit.

Practical Uses: Cherry wood is a hard and prized wood for making furniture. It can also be used for toys and musical instruments.

Conservation: Climate change is causing cherry trees to blossom earlier than usual. It has knock-down effects on the ecosystem, including animals and insects.

Cherry Tree Magic—Love Spell with Cherry Fruit

To attract lasting love, use cherry tree magic to bring true love. Rose quartz brings the vibration of love to the spell.

You will need

+ A fresh piece of linen, six-to-eight-inch round or square
+ 9 dried cherry pits (preferably from cherry fruit you have consumed)
+ Heart-shaped icon, charm, or stone
+ Rose quartz stone
+ Pen or marker—preferable pink or red
+ 2 pieces of red ribbon or string, twelve inches each

Directions:

1. Center yourself.

2. Fill your mind with thoughts of love and visualize your prospective partner. Think energetically and not physically. What does it *feel* like to be with this person?

3. On the inside of the piece of linen, at the center, draw two hearts intertwined or linked.

4. Pick up two cherry seeds. Place them in the center of the hearts and say, "*I place this pair to represent true and mutual love.*" Pick up two more seeds and say, "*I place this pair for balanced exchange.*" Pick up two more and say, "*I place these seeds for truth and loyalty.*" Pick up two more seeds and say, "*I place this pair for health and endurance.*" Pick up the last seed and say, "*I place this seed for the everlasting bond that unites us. May it stay strong for all eternity.*" Take the rose quartz stone and the heart icon and place them with the cherry pits and say, "*May this union be created and blessed by all the gods, goddesses, guides, and entities that bring two hearts together in love.*" Close the placement by saying "*Amen,*" or any other phrase you prefer.

5. Bring the sides or corners together and tie up the bundle with the first ribbon or string. Tie the second ribbon to the bundle as a loop for hanging.

6. Either hang the bundle in a place where you can see it daily or under your bed or pillow.

7. When you see it every day, bless it and know it works on your behalf.

Chestnut *(Castanea sativa or Dentata)*

Chestnut (*Castanea sativa or Dentata*)

Chestnut trees have been cultivated and used for their edible nuts since 2000 BCE. The nuts have been a valuable source of food for humans. They are starchy and used to make flour and a potato look-alike dish. In modern times, nine different types of chestnut trees grow in temperate areas worldwide.

Chestnut trees grow to be a hundred feet high. They were a favorite of Romans in the sixteenth century and developed into a European favorite. An old Corsican wedding tradition says to prepare twenty-two different chestnut dishes and serve them on the wedding day (FineDiningGlovers.com 2013).

Don't mistake the *Castanea* version for the *Aesculus* version because the horse chestnuts from the *Aesculus* tree are not edible and can be poisonous to humans, livestock, horses, and other animals.

In George Orwell's *1984*, the chestnut tree is used in poems recited throughout, referring to nature, modern life, or the saying: "that old chestnut." There's also a bar where the protagonist Winston Smith goes called the Chestnut Tree Café (FineDiningGlovers.com 2013).

Symbolism: Life, fertility, birth, sustenance
It is called the "bread tree" from ancient times.

Essential Oil: Chestnut oil is obtained from the kernel of the chestnut. Chestnut is also known as horse chestnut. It is native to the northern hemisphere. Horse chestnut is lethal if consumed raw.

Gemstone: Brown sea jasper—responsibility, nurturing, healing of lower chakras

Magic: Chestnuts are said to encourage fertility and conception. It is also a tree of peace, calm, and protection. If you want to bless a new home, place a bowl of sweet chestnuts in each room of the new home to attract prosperity, abundance, and harmony. Chestnut wood placed under the bed of a fighting couple will encourage bonding and rekindle love.

Notable Associations: Zeus and the Druid shamans, who made staffs from its wood

Medicine: Chestnuts are the only nuts that contain vitamin C. Half a cup of raw chestnuts gives you 35 to 45 percent of your daily intake of vitamin C. They contain antioxidants and provide many vitamins and minerals. They can be used for digestion improvement and bone loss prevention.

> Chestnuts are the only nuts that contain vitamin C. Half a cup of raw chestnuts gives you 35 to 45 percent of your daily intake of vitamin C.

Caution: Only four types of chestnuts are suitable for human consumption: Japanese chestnut, American chestnut, Chinese chestnut, and European chestnut. Avoid all others—especially the horse chestnut.

Practical Uses: Chestnuts are great for making cakes and brews. *Castagnaccio* is the name of a plain chestnut flour cake, typical of Tuscany and Liguria. Mont Blanc is a dessert of puréed, sweetened chestnuts topped with whipped cream, a huge favorite of Cesare and Lucrezia Borgia. Breweries in France, Central Europe, and Brazil make chestnut beer. A brewer in St. Louis, Missouri, has begun making American chestnut beer.

Due to its high tannin content, chestnut tree poles are used for telephone poles, fire logs, and poles for vineyards.

Conservation: During the first half of the twentieth century, a devastating fungal disease was accidentally introduced into the North American ecosystem through imported Japanese chestnut trees. It is classified as endangered. The horse chestnut is also classified as vulnerable to extinction due to the ravaging of the trees by moths. About half of the trees face disappearance from the natural landscape.

Chestnut Tree Magic—Blessing for a New Home

Moving into a new home is always a special occasion, and with friends and loved ones gathered around, a great opportunity to bless both the house and its new occupants. It is also a good time to "clean house" of any past energies that no longer belong there and make room for the new family and its happy future. Use chestnut tree magic for protection, abundance, and harmony.

You will need:

+   A small bowl of chestnuts for each room you want to bless

+   A 4 oz. mister or small spray bottle filled with 4 drops of rosemary essential oil, ½ teas alcohol, witch hazel, or vodka, and 3 oz. spring water, shaken well (rosemary essential oil is known for purification because of the ketones and monoterpenes, which expunge toxins)

Directions

You will walk from room to room.

Opening statement:
What a happy day this is! (Names of new homeowners) *are moving into their new home, and we are here to celebrate and bless this wonderful new beginning.*

This is an exciting time, the start of a new adventure and their lives together under this roof. A family will learn and grow within these walls, and we all wish for years of peace, safety, and happiness here.

We will place a bowl of chestnuts in each room to signify harmony, attract prosperity, and shower the new residents with abundance and love.

Spritz/mist twice into the air of each room, place the bowl of chestnuts in the room, and say:

In the kitchen:
May the food prepared in this room always nourish those who eat here. May it build strong bodies and inspire wise and peaceful minds, and may there always be plenty in this house.

In the bedroom:

May love abide here. May the day end gently here. May the nights be peaceful, and may sleep come easily. And may every morning be welcomed with a smile of gratitude for another day of love and joy and prosperity for this family.

In the family room:

Life happens here. This family room is dedicated to the growth of this family in every area of their lives. May they come to greater understanding of the unique gifts of each of the members of this family, and may they grow in love within these walls, and may that love reach beyond these walls to touch and bless the lives of others.

Closing Statement:

This is a new beginning. Today we cleanse and bless this house of all remnants of the past so it may be free to provide only blessings for this family.

May times of joy be multiplied many times over. May opportunities abound within these walls, and may the occasional moments of sadness, sorrow, or concern be washed away by the tears of love and the soothing sound of laughter.

Amen, or however you close your prayers.

Coconut *(Cocos nucifera L.)*

Coconut (*Cocos nucifera L.*)

Coconut trees come in dwarf and tall. Dwarf coconut trees can reach sixty feet high, while tall coconut trees grow ninety-eight feet tall. The fruit is called *drupe* and matures in one year. Coconut trees produce roots that expand as far out horizontally as they are tall.

Coconuts grow in coastal tropical regions and are a cultural icon of tropical destinations. But they can also be grown indoors in an atrium setting. It's interesting that coconuts only sprout from their seed. You can't graft a tree or use cuttings. The nuts are ready to be planted when they make a "sloshing" sound when shaken.

Sinbad the sailor was said to have bought and sold coconuts on his voyage. I'm curious to know what he did with all those shells after eating the coconuts at sea.

Symbolism: The coconut is called *The Tree of Life* because it produces shelter, food, and liquid for humans and animals. It represents purity and healing.

Essential Oil: Coconut oil is pressed from the meat of the coconut. The oil pressed from fresh, unprocessed coconut "meat" is called "virgin." "Refined" coconut oil is made from dried coconut meat and "fractionated," meaning it has been heated beyond its melting point. Fractionation keeps the oil in liquid form.

Gemstone: Moonstone—intuition, psychic abilities, compassion, and clairvoyance

Magic: Whole coconuts are broken to dispel black magic cast on a person. They are used in India to replace human and animal sacrifices to the gods.

> Whole coconuts are broken to dispel black magic cast on a person. They are used in India to replace human and animal sacrifices to the gods.

Notable Associations: Brahma, Vishnu, and Mahesh

Medicine: Coconut is an important part of the human diet because it contains valuable vitamins and minerals. Coconut water, meat, sugar, and oil have fed many humans for millennia.

Caution: Used daily coconut oil can give you diarrhea and gut issues.

Practical Uses: The wooden parts of coconut trees are used for making furniture, decorative objects, drums, and canoes. Many people use coconut oil for cooking, hair, and cosmetics. Coconut oil can be a substitute for diesel oil. The hard shells can be used for fuel and fire after the fruit is extracted.

Conservation: The coconut tree is endangered worldwide. Lethal *yellowing diseases* are spreading and producing a global pandemic for *cocos nucifera*. With high demand for oils, sugars, milk, amino, flours, and fruit, the market is increasing while the coconut trees are diminishing.

Coffee *(Coffea)*

Coffee (*Coffea*)

Coffea is a generous genus with more than ninety species of flowering plants in the Rubiaceae family. They can be shrubs or small trees and are classically native to subtropical Africa and southern Asia. Seeds of several species are the source of the popular beverage coffee.

The *coffea* plant produces multicolored "cherries" ranging from green to red to yellow. The coffee "bean" is the seed of the cherry. This seed must be removed from the covering of the cherry and dried before ending up in someone's breakfast cup.

Coffee, as we know and love it, is made from the seeds of the Arabica or Robusta plants. Arabica trees are grown in steep terrains and must be cultivated at specific temperatures. They make up 70 percent of the world's coffee beans. Robusta plants make up 30 percent of the world's coffee and are cultivated and grown in areas with a lot of rainfall. Robusta has more caffeine than Arabica.

The coffee tree fruit can be affected by climate conditions, elevation, soil, seeds, cultivation of the plant/tree, and varying latitudes. Latitudes affect the time of harvest, and elevations affect the acidity or sweetness of the seeds.

For centuries, coffee had been a huge mystery in Europe. But, by the seventeenth century, this dark, earthy drink found its way to the continent and became a hit. The new "invention" brewed foes who called it "the bitter invention of Satan" and thought it to be pure corruption. However, in 1615, Pope Clement VIII accepted an offer to try a hot coffee drink before making the final spiritual decision. He sipped. He liked. Then he baptized the beans to become Christianized and therefore no longer under Satan's prefecture.

Symbolism: Emotions, changes, transformation, friendship, balance

Essential Oil: Coffee blossom essential oil is extracted from the pillowy white blossoms of the coffee plant. It is antiseptic, anti-inflammatory, and astringent.

Gemstone: Brown tourmaline—gentle soothing of all emotions, relaxation for matters of the heart

Magic: Use coffee to focus your thoughts and intentions. Place coffee on the sacred space to deepen and intensify all spells, blessings, and protections. Coarsely ground coffee beans made into a nighttime eye mask or pillow will help remove headaches and nightmares. Offer the deities you work with a cup of coffee as a sign of your firm intentions. Use coffee as blessing water to spritz on amulets or spell icons. Coffee will add speed to your spells and affirmations when used in rituals. Use coffee essential oil to awaken the senses, help with respiration, and as a natural skin anti-ager when applied (diluted) to the face.

> Place a small amount of coffee in your sacred space to deepen and intensify all spells, blessings, and protections.

Notable Associations: Caffeina

Medicine: The properties in coffee are: addictive, analeptic, analgesic, aphrodisiacal, anorexic, anti-emetic, anti-soporific, an antidote to narcotics, cardiotonic (increases blood flow), cholegogue, counter-irritant, diuretic (loses its effect with continued use), hypnotic, increases peristalsis, intellectual aid, nervine, and a stimulant (Leonard 2021).

Caution: There are harmful effects of coffee. More than four cups of coffee per day is linked to an early death. A Mayo Clinic partnered study found that men who drank more than four eight-ounce cups of coffee had a 21 percent increase in all-cause mortality.

Practical Uses: The wood of the coffee tree is valued for its rich color and dense grain. It is used for furniture, cabinets, interior millwork. Coffee grounds have innumerable uses, including fertilizing gardens and bringing nutrients such as nitrogen, calcium, potassium, iron, phosphorus, magnesium, and chromium. They also attract worms to the garden, and coffee grounds repel bugs, making compost richer and better.

> Coffee grounds placed in your garden soil can help with fertilization, supplying nutrients such as nitrogen, calcium, potassium, iron, phosphorus, magnesium, chromium, and micronutrients such as magnesium, copper, and calcium.

Conservation: In the 1900s, the coffee industry began deforesting millions of acres of rich, bio-diverse rainforest to increase production and profits. They began switching to sun-grown farming methods to produce larger trees with higher yields in high density. The environmental impact has been devastating. Sun-grown coffee requires more fertilizers and cuts the lifespan of a coffee tree in half. This has proven to be an unsustainable model as the industry grapples with finding the right balance of shade and sun (Wauters 2021).

Cottonwood *(Populus)*

Cottonwood *(Populus)*

The cottonwood tree grows and spreads and is a favorite for landscaping and shade. It grows so fast that it is desirable for planting in areas prone to flooding and soil erosion. It is also known as a poplar tree.

The cottonwood tree blooms in the early spring with five-pointed star-shaped flowers. Native Americans believed that the seeds of the cottonwood tree burst forth in spring to scatter the skies with stars.

The legend goes, "The spirit of the wind knew the stars were hiding in the twigs of the cottonwood tree, and so it created a mighty gale that would snap the branches from the trees. As the branches broke and fell to the ground, the stars shot out of the tree into the sky" (Guthrie 2014).

The flowers of the cottonwood tree, called catkins, hang as dangling clusters and bloom in April and May. The cotton-looking masses on the tree are the wind-borne seeds. The tree grows six feet a year and can reach up to a hundred feet.

The cottonwood is common in North America, Europe, and some parts of Asia. They thrive in wetlands and arid soil while providing cheap timber.

The cottonwood tree grows thick bark and makes a good form of protection against heat and fire—it can also survive the onslaught of droughts and forest fires.

Symbolism: Hope, healing and transformation, ancient wisdom, ancestor connection

Essential Oil: Cottonwood oil is rich in balsamic resin, a topical anti-inflammatory. It is also used as an analgesic and anti-inflammatory herbal oil.

Gemstone: Polished selenite—peace, calm, mental clarity, connection with the higher realms

Magic: The cottonwood tree invites us to reconnect with ancient wisdom and helps us pierce the veil to our ancestors. We cannot embrace the future without connecting to the past. A Sun Dance Ceremony connects us to the past. If you break a cottonwood tree twig at the right place, you will find a shadow where a star once hid.

Notable Associations: Hecate, and the goddess Nienna, chief guardian of the souls of the dead, who helps them make their journeys between worlds into their new lives.

> The cottonwood tree invites us to reconnect with ancient wisdom and helps us pierce the veil to our ancestors. We cannot embrace the future without connecting to the past.

Medicine: Cottonwood tree bark was medicine for Native Americans. Cottonwood bud oil and salve is used as a multi-purpose healer for achy joints, carpal tunnel syndrome, and burns. The buds and bark of the cottonwood tree contain salicin that breaks down into salicylic acid or aspirin. Add to oil and it could be used for pain relief, fever, or inflammation.

Caution: Cottonwood products are not for ingestion.

Practical Uses: Native Americans dug out cottonwood trees and made canoes. The wood is good for burning but must be seasoned correctly to prevent a putrid odor from coming out of wood that is too green. Cottonwood is a soft hardwood, but it can be good for shelving, framing, paneling, subfloors, crates, pallets, lowboy decks, saddles, and caskets.

Conservation: In Massachusetts, swamp cottonwood is listed as endangered under the Massachusetts Endangered Species Act, as is black poplar, due to habitat destruction.

Cypress *(Cupressus)*

Cypress *(Cupressus)*

The Persians believe this was the first tree to grow in paradise due to its evergreen nature. Cypress trees are often eighty feet high and grow in a pyramidal shape, reaching upward. Cypress trees are the only trees that have knees, little knobs that form on the tree as woody growths. The tree is both deciduous and a conifer, meaning its seeds are cones.

Symbolism: Immortality, protection, longevity, past lives

Cypress represents souls moving to the celestial realm. It is the symbol of everlasting life and can be found planted near ancient cemeteries. Use it as protection and for longevity. Ancients made crowns of cypress to honor the god Pluto, the ruler of the underworld.

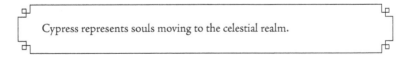

Cypress represents souls moving to the celestial realm.

Essential Oil: Cypress oil is an essential oil made from the cypress tree's twigs, stems, and leaves. Cypress oil has many health benefits, including antibacterial, antimicrobial, and antifungal properties.

Gemstone: Green jade—manifestation, peace, harmony, good fortune, longevity

Magic: Place cypress branches on the graves of the departed to help them on their journey. Wearing a twig of cypress at a funeral helps the departed have an easier journey. Use cypress essential oil for meditation to attract longevity and prosperity.

Notable Associations: Hades, Apollo, Artemis, Astarte, Athena

Medicine: Cypress contains terpenes. It has been used as an ointment for head colds, coughs, bronchitis, hemorrhoids, and varicose veins.

Caution: Do not use if pregnant or breastfeeding. Bleeding disorders could worsen with cypress. Stop using cypress two weeks before surgery. Test for allergic reaction before using.

Practical Uses: According to the Old Testament, the cypress tree was used for shipbuilding and the erection of Solomon's temple. The strong wood was used for beams in buildings, wooden floors, and musical instruments. It is valued for its longevity and resistance to rot. In the 1700s, it was used for giant canoes and water pipes. It has been used to make roofing shingles, railroad ties, ladders, fence posts, and siding for homes. Today, cypress is still harvested, and more than 50 percent is used as lumber, while about 47 percent is chipped and sold as mulch (Leschmann 2017).

Conservation: Some varieties of cypress are endangered: the Laos cypress, the bald cypress, the berg cypress, the African cypress, and the almost extinct swamp cypress.

Dogwood Tree (*Cornus*)

Dogwood Tree (*Cornus*)

There are over fifty species within the *Cornus*, or dogwood, genus. The trees grow well by streams and rivers but do not thrive where the soil is overly moist. It is advised to plant your dogwood trees in places where the deer cannot reach the tree because it is irresistible to some wildlife. The name dogwood comes from the word "dog-tree," introduced into English in 1548. Shakespeare wrote of the tree in reference to Hecate in *Macbeth*.

Thomas Jefferson made the dogwood tree famous. They flourished on his Monticello estate in Virginia and wooed the state decision-makers to pick dogwood as its official state flower.

Many states followed suit, and dogwood festivals are held in the South in the spring and are cause for annual celebrations. The dogwood is the state flower of Missouri. North Carolina and Virginia made it their state flower and tree.

Symbolism: Stealth, wishes, secrets, loyalty, protection.
The four-petal blossom represents the four directions: NESW.

Essential Oil: Dogwood oil is available from some private distillers. However, the quality and purity of private distillation and extraction cannot be guaranteed. Clary sage (*Salvia sclarea L*) is a compatible essential oil.

Gemstone: Polished snow quartz—clarity, innocence, and connecting with higher self

Magic: Dogwood is also thought to derive from "dagwood," which used the tree's thin twigs to create daggers back in ancient times. Wands, arrows, spears, and daggers came from this tree. If a maiden in the Middle Ages was given a dogwood bouquet, it meant the suitor was interested. If she returned it, she was saying she wasn't interested. If she kept it, she was encouraging his advances. Place the sap of the dogwood onto a handkerchief on Midsummer Eve. It will grant your wishes if you carry it faithfully.

> Place the sap of the dogwood onto a handkerchief on Midsummer Eve. It will grant your wishes if you carry it with you faithfully.

Notable Associations: Hecate

Medicine: Dogwood bark is rich in tannins. The bark or leaves are ground and treat pain, fevers, backaches, headaches, dizziness, weakness, excessive sweating, uterine bleeding, and incontinence. Some use it to treat boils.

Caution: There is not enough evidence to say if dogwood products are safe to use. Definitely not during pregnancy and not to be confused with Jamaican dogwood, which is poisonous.

Practical Uses: Dogwood is a hard wood. It is used for golf club heads, textile shuttles, bows (archery), mallets, pulleys, and turned objects. It is also used for furniture, but it is hard to work with. Older trees present colors and textures, but the young trees do not.

Conservation: The dogwood is at risk for fungus and pest infestations. For this reason, it is critical to buy a sapling from an arborist instead of transplanting the tree from the wild.

Elder *(Sambucus nigra)*

Elder *(Sambucus nigra)*

The elder has a variety of disguises. Common names include elder, elderberry, black elder, European elder, European elderberry, and European black elderberry. It thrives in various climate conditions, including wet and dry fertile soils. It is a sun-lover and can be poisonous to mammals.

Ogham: Letter R—Ruis

Symbolism: Transformation, death, regeneration, healing, protection

Of all the Ogham trees, it has strong fairy connections, witch superstitions, and magical protection. Elder represents the end of a cycle or problem and signals a rebirth. The Elder Mother is said to live within this tree.

Essential Oil: Elderflower essential oil comes from a plant and not the tree.

Gemstone: Tree agate—inner stability, balance, even distribution

Magic: Elder will help with exorcism and ridding a person of a curse or evil spell. Elder is associated with the number thirteen. It is believed witches can turn themselves into elder trees. Druids used it to shapeshift. Cut twigs at the full moon, wrap them in red thread, infuse them with magical intention, and wear them around your neck. An elder planted by your home will keep the devil away. Judas is believed to have hung himself on an elder tree after his betrayal. In Denmark, the elder is deeply connected with magic.

Elder is associated with the number thirteen. It is believed witches can turn themselves into elder trees. Druids used it to shapeshift. The elder is deeply connected with magic.

Notable Associations: Venus, Loki, Hel, Hela, Holda, Hilde

Medicine: Elderberries are full of vitamin C. Elder tree tea can help purify blood and treat coughs and an irritated throat. It can be used as a skin toner and lotion. Chemists can make ear drops, eye drops, and skin lotions. Leaves can be used as compresses on surface wounds.

Caution: The berries and raw leaves should never be consumed. Excess elder tea could cause nausea, vomiting, and diarrhea. The flowers and berries are mildly poisonous, so they should be cooked before eating.

Practical Uses: The bark, roots, and berries can be used as a natural dye. Mature wood is good for whittling and carving. The wood is hard and has been used for combs, spindles, and pegs, and the hollow stems have been fashioned into flutes and blowguns.

Conservation: The red-berried elderberry is on the endangered list. The Valley Elderberry Longhorn Beetle is listed as a threatened species under the federal Endangered Species Act, although it is not a tree but shares the name.

Elm (Ulmus)

Elm (*Ulmus*)

If there was one perfect tree, it might be the elm. The genus was existed twenty million years ago and has been around in ancient cultures since then. The tree features graceful, vase-shaped spreading branches and features oval, tooth-edged green leaves with points. It has been used as a decoration for public places for centuries. There was a discussion between the king of England and the king of France at Gisors, Normandy, France, in 1188. The English king stood under the elm in the shade during the discussions while the king of France stood in the hot sun. After the exchanges, the sunburnt king of France ordered the elm chopped down. The innocent elm received the brunt of the French king's displeasure regarding shade. Now, nobody gets the shade!

The elm is a hardwood tree and was popular in the US in the 1900s. Many people planted them in urban centers and to line city streets. Then, tragedy struck, and the elm suffered from Dutch Elm Disease in the midcentury, which wiped out much of the elm tree population.

Symbolism: Nobility, open mindedness, communication, relationships, feminine power

Essential Oil: Elm tree essential oil is available. However, the quality and purity of private distillation and extraction cannot be guaranteed. Comparable essential oil is rosemary (*Rosmarinus officinalis L.*).

Gemstone: Chrysoprase—joy, happiness, new love, prosperity, abundance

Magic: If you wish to meet fairies, sit in an elm grove at dawn and sing soft, melodic tunes. You will be joined by the wee people. The elm represents the dark side of the psyche. Elm wood was found at the crossroads to the fairy world. It made coffins for the ancient Greeks. Elm represents endurance, fertility, the passage through death into rebirth, and holds stability and grounding for the user. Wands made of elm are fairy wands.

> Elm wood was found at the crossroads to the fairy world. If you wish to meet fairies, sit in an elm grove at dawn and sing soft, melodic tunes. You will be joined by the wee people.

Notable Associations: Dionysus, Hades, Orpheus, Odin, Lodr, Woden

Medicine: An infusion is made of the root bark and has treated coughs, colds, and excessive menstruation. A special decoction has been used as an eyewash, and the inner bark has been used as an emollient for tumors. Native Americans have used the bark for curing wounds, boils, ulcers, and skin inflammations, and it may also be able to help with coughs, sore throats, stomach problems, and diarrhea (Devaney 2010).

Caution: There is not enough evidence to label elm medicine as safe. Especially pregnant or breastfeeding women should not use without their physician's approval.

Practical Uses: Elm wood is excellent for butcher block tops and cutting boards because it is odorless, has interlocking grains, and won't split. Immersed in water, elm is resistant to decay; it is used in boatbuilding, making wagon wheels, chairs, coffins, and planking. Today, elm wood is used in manufacturing but is difficult to find in retail outlets. It is used for furniture, crates, and boxes. Elm was the choice for ancient longbows, keels, and Japanese Taiko drums.

Conservation: Many elm species are susceptible to Dutch Elm Disease, a devastating fungoid disease spread by bark beetles. Dutch Elm Disease has drastically reduced wild and cultivated elm populations throughout Europe and North America. Some species are also vulnerable to elm phloem necrosis. Resistant strains are preferred for planting (Britannica.com 2021).

Seedlings are being cultivated to be disease resistant, and the elm population may once again populate the earth.

Eucalyptus *(Eucalyptus)*

Eucalyptus (*Eucalyptus*)

There are more than eight hundred varieties of the Eucalyptus genus, including tall trees and shrubs. They are part of the myrtle family (*Myrtaceae*).

The eucalypti are gum trees and hail from Australia, Tasmania, and nearby islands. They grow to sixty feet in height and are the main food source for the beloved koala bear.

They are fast-growing trees with resilient and durable lumber. The wood burns well, and the oils produced by the leaves have been a universal medicine to the Aboriginal tribes for centuries. It got its name "tea tree" because English explorer Captain James Cook first made tea from the tree leaves before taking samples of it back to England in 1770.

It is the tallest flowering gum tree on earth. However, it is also a dangerous tree because the leaves are loaded with oil and, in a firestorm, can explode.

Symbolism: Division of Earth and heaven, purification, cleansing, healing

Essential Oil: Steam distilled from the eucalyptus tree, it has the properties of eucalyptol and alpha-terpineol, which aid with respiratory conditions. There are many varieties of eucalypts; choose the oil from the varietal that suits your needs.

Gemstone: Australian chrysoprase—happiness, enterprise, prudence
Moonstone—intuition, psychic abilities, compassion, and clairvoyance

Magic: The eucalyptus is a holy tree for the Aboriginal people. Negative energy disappears the moment you burn a leaf. Use the leaves or essential oil for cleansing sacred spaces like temples, churches, homes, and oneself.

Notable Associations: Moon, Artemis, Mawu, Selene

Medicine: Used for nasal congestion, bronchial congestion, tick spray, wound cleansing, acne, and skin infections.

Caution: Never consume tea tree oil internally. (No matter what anyone tells you!) It can cause serious symptoms such as confusion, ataxia (loss of muscle coordination), breathing problems, and coma.

Practical Uses: Eucalyptus is resistant to rot, so it is used to construct buildings, outdoor furniture, and household accessories.

Conservation: A global assessment of all 826 known species of eucalypt trees—of which 812 grow only in Australia—has found almost a quarter are threatened with extinction. *Eucalyptus copulans* is a critically endangered tree in the Blue Mountains of New South Wales.

Eucalyptus Tree Magic—Clearing Negative Energy

Eucalyptus magic can turn any space from a place of negativity into a bastion of peace, love, and joy. It brings fresh, clean energy on board.

You will need:

✦ Eucalyptus leaves or a eucalyptus smudge stick

✦ A burning bowl

✦ A lighting tool

✦ A small bell

✦ A small spray bottle (4 oz.) filled with 4 drops of eucalyptus essential oil, ½ teaspoon alcohol, witch hazel, or vodka, and 3 oz spring water, shaken well

Directions

1. Carry the spritzer bottle of essential oil, your smudge stick, lighted (or your burning bowl of eucalyptus leaves if you can carry it safely) and your bell with you.

2. Begin at the front door and walk left to right through the house.

3. In each room, walk through the room, holding the burning eucalyptus smudge stick or smoking bowl. Say: *"I cleanse this room from any and all past negative experiences and memories."* Spritz the air with the essential oil. Say, *"I purify this room for new beginnings and fresh energy."* Now, ring your bell and say, *"And so it is,"* or any other phrase of conclusion you prefer.

4. Do this for every room to cleanse the whole house.

5. This is a wonderful practice for preparing a new home, a new relationship, after a soul departs, following a divorce or a breakup. Anytime change occurs and negativity remains, use this ritual for a fresh beginning.

Fig (*Ficus carica*)

Fig (*Ficus carica*)

We have all seen the statues of Adam and Eve covering themselves with fig leaves as their first designer clothing in the Garden of Eden. The fig was also mentioned in Deuteronomy 8:8, where the Promised Land is described as "a land of wheat and barley, of vines and fig trees and pomegranates" (Top Verses of the Bible/Deuteronomy 2007).

The fig has had fame and importance for many centuries. It is a pantropical species. We think of it as a fruit, but it is a *syconium*. The fig tree can live for a hundred years and grow to fifty feet. Trees flourish in hot, dry, arid climates because the syconium needs the potent, all-day sun to ripen.

The oldest known living tree planting is the *Ficus religiosa*, known as the Sri Maha Bodhi, planted at Buddha Gaya in India. It is the tree under which Buddha sat and attained Enlightenment. It was planted in 288 BCE.

Symbolism: Fertility, protection, sacredness, enlightenment, strength. The Romans held the fig sacred, and the Buddhists view it as enlightenment.

Essential Oil: Fig oil is available as a fig fragrance oil. However, the quality and purity of private distillation and extraction cannot be guaranteed. Compatible oil is pomegranate (*Punica granatum L.*).

Gemstone: Ruby fuchsite—courage, strength, emotional support

Magic: Used for fertility rituals, male potency, spiritual enlightenment, and sacred practices.

Notable Associations: Dionysus, Mars (Demeter is said to have given the fig to Dionysus), Brahma, Shiva, Nirantali

Medicine: High in potassium, iron, fiber, and plant calcium, figs are also used for medicinal purposes as a diuretic and laxative and made into syrups for cough. The fig leaf is used for diabetes, high cholesterol, and skin conditions. Some people have been known to apply the milky sap (latex) from the tree directly to the skin to treat skin tumors and warts.

Caution: Skin contact with fig fruit or leaves can cause rashes in sensitive people. Some people may have allergic reactions. Do not use fig two weeks before surgery.

Practical Uses: Fig wood contains latex and therefore can be a toxin. Fig trees don't grow straight, so wooden planks are not straight. They are too twisted and curved to be used in buildings or furniture. The wood is soft and not reliable for construction.

Conservation: The fig tree itself is not endangered. It is used to save other endangered species, like the fructivores in Borneo.

Fir (*Abies*)

Fir (*Abies*)

Fir means any species of conifers belonging to the genus *Abies*, which is included in the pine, *Pinaceae*, family. These large trees can be distinguished from other conifers by noting their soft cones that perch upright like candles on the branches. We are familiar with the fir tree, Douglas fir, especially as being the prototype for the Christmas Tree. There are fifty-six identified species of the fir tree.

The fir tree can grow from 33 feet to 250 feet. They mostly grow in mountainous regions and can live over five hundred years. Monarch butterflies live in fir trees.

Fir was one of the nine sacred trees of the Druids and burned in the holy fires of Samhain and Beltane.

Ogham: Letter A—Ailm

Symbolism: Protection, spirituality, honesty, truth, youth, vitality, immortality.

Essential Oil: Several fir needle oils are available: Balsam, Douglas, Siberian, Grand. Choose the ones with the properties you desire for respiration, congestion, immune support, muscle aches, stiff or painful joints, antibacterial cleansing, and energizing.

Gemstone: Green sea jasper—balance, healing, heart-opening

Magic: Incense, essential oil, and dried fir needles can work for spells and rituals. Fir needles can be burned at childbirth to bless and protect both mother and baby. Fir resin is a magical seal for a spell. Fir is the scent of memories and transport one into a past life. It is a wonderful tool to bring prosperity.

> Fir is the scent of memories and can be used to transport one into a past life.

Notable Associations: Dionysus, Thor, Osiris, Bel, Bacchus

Medicine: Fir essential oil extracted from the needles and used externally is helpful for coughs, colds, flu, arthritis, muscle aches, and rheumatism. It is an antiseptic, antitussive, deodorant, disinfectant, and expectorant.

A tea high in vitamins A and C can be made from green fir needles steeped in boiling water.

Caution: Avoid using during pregnancy. Never take silver fir essential oil internally. For safety, ecologically dispose of old or oxidized oils.

Practical Uses: The dense grain of the fir wood makes it ideal for use in construction. However, the wood is not disease- or decay-resistant and therefore should only be used indoors unless treated for the duration. It is used for flooring, windows, panels, trim, doors, and plywood. Dried correctly, it is excellent for burning in fires.

Conservation: Douglas fir in the Pacific Northwest has been stricken with horrendous fungal disease, Rhabdocline and Swiss Needlecast, the likes of which can devastate a natural landscape.

Mexican authorities list the Colima fir tree (*Abies colimensis*) as an endangered species. Its survival has been threatened by logging and, more recently, by fires to clear the land for the orchards that follow.

The Fraser fir is endangered in its habitat. Acid rain and the *woolly adelgid* are taking a high toll on naturally occurring stands of Fraser fir.

Chapter Eight

Magical Trees G–M

Magical Trees

G–M

- ◆ Ginkgo
- ◆ Hawthorn
- ◆ Hazel
- ◆ Hemlock
- ◆ Holly
- ◆ Jacaranda
- ◆ Juniper
- ◆ Lemon
- ◆ Linden
- ◆ Mahogany
- ◆ Magnolia
- ◆ Maple
- ◆ Mulberry
- ◆ Myrtle

Gingko (*Gingko biloba*)

Gingko (*Gingko biloba*)

Ginkgo biloba is also known by ginkgo or gingko, and as the *maidenhair* tree. The tree dates back two hundred million years, and the gingko is the only remaining non-extinct species in its class. It is a member of an ancient genus, having fossils dating back two hundred million years.

It is both a shade and an ornamental tree and has beautiful fan-shaped leaves that turn a breathtaking yellow in the fall. The best part is that it establishes itself nicely in most climates, including urban dwellings. Streets are lined with ginkgo trees because they are hardy and can withstand the salting from snow control, pet waste, cold, and wind, while many other species can't withstand these urban tortures.

What's fascinating about the ginkgo is that it is called a *living fossil* because it has not changed in two hundred million years. Imagine that! This tree coexisted with dinosaurs.

The downside is that it has incredibly smelly seed pods. But, if you're brave enough to open them, the seeds are delicious. However, they are mildly toxic, so a few is all you get.

Symbolism: Magic, longevity, fertility, prosperity.

Essential Oil: Gingko Biloba essential oil is available. However, the quality and purity of private distillation and extraction cannot be guaranteed. A compatible essential oil is Helichrysum.

Gemstone: Yellow jade—energetic, stimulating, brings joy and happiness

Magic: Plant a gingko tree at the birth of the child to ensure longevity. Plant a gingko tree when someone dies to assist their peaceful journey and existence in the afterlife. Use the leaves for fertility rituals and use any part of the tree— seeds, bark, pods, or leaves—to work any kind of magic spell. The ancient wisdom will be passed to you.

> Plant a gingko tree to honor someone who has died and to assist them in their peaceful journey into the afterlife and beyond.

Notable Associations: Venus

Medicine: Peter Crane says, "In China, it's mainly the seeds that are used. Yet, the *Ginkgo biloba* that you buy in health food stores here [USA] is an extract of the leaves" (Cohn 2013). Dried ginkgo leaves have been used for centuries in traditional Chinese medicine to ease lung ailments and improve circulation. In the US, we use it for memory. The leaves contain flavones, glycosides, lactones, sitosterol, bio flavones, and anthocyanins. These compounds relax the blood vessels and stimulate the circulatory system. It is believed that Ginkgo improves mental function because it improves blood flow in the brain. This ancient healing tree is being examined in ongoing medical research to treat vascular disorders, memory loss, and the overall effects of aging.

Caution: Gingko Biloba potency can vary from one manufacturer to another. Be careful of taking this product. Doctors recommend caution when taking this herb, as it is extremely potent.

Practical Uses: The wood of Ginkgo biloba is used to make furniture, chessboards, carving, and caskets for making sake; the wood is fire-resistant and slow to decay.

Conservation: Ginkgo Biloba was once widespread throughout the world. However, only two populations are found to grow in the wild today in the Tian Mu Shan Reserve, the Zhejiang province in eastern China. For centuries, it was thought to be extinct in the wild. Although these two populations naturally occur in the wild, they show an important genetic uniformity, suggesting that these groves were planted and cared for by Tibetan or Chinese monks for thousands of years.

The Ginkgo Biloba tree has been propagated throughout the centuries and is now cultivated worldwide. Despite that, the International Union for the Conservation of Nature Red List of Threatened Species (above) lists Ginkgo Biloba as an endangered species because of its rarity in the wild (Chen 2013).

Hawthorn *(Crataegus)*

Hawthorn *(Crataegus)*

The hawthorn, *Crataegus,* comprises hundreds of species in the rose family (*Rosaceae*). The trees grow fifteen to fifty feet tall and eight to thirty-five feet wide, depending on the variety. They are planted in gardens and dot the landscape of ancient Celtic lands. The hawthorn was celebrated for its beauty, ability to sustain life and was revered and feared due to its fairy connection.

The trees provide fragrant white or pink five-petaled flowers resembling apple blossoms, and the fruits look like rose hips. They bloom in various colors— red, orange, yellow, or black. The edible fruit is classified as pomes, like apples and pears, and produced in fall and last through the winter. They have various culinary and medicinal qualities and serve as a food source for robins, waxwings, and other songbirds.

The hawthorn tree has enchanting blossoms and long thorns, which the blossoms disguise. The thorns can scrape and puncture, causing infection and allergic reaction.

In England, the hawthorn is called the mayflower because it blooms in May. Is it an interesting coincidence that the first pilgrim ship to America was also named the *Mayflower?* Certain sections of the UK are named after the hawthorn: *Woodmansterne* (Surrey) "thorn on the edge of a wood"; *Appleton Thorn* (Cheshire); *Hatherdene* (Hampshire) "hawthorn valley"; *Hathern,* (Leicestershire) "hawthorn."

It is alleged that when Joseph of Arimathea came to Glastonbury, England, he stuck his staff (reported to be Jesus' staff) in the ground on Wearyall Hill, and it immediately sprang into a hawthorn tree. It lived for two thousand years until vandals chopped it down in 2010. The destruction was viewed as an attack on Christianity.

Ogham: The Letter H—Huath

Symbolism: Renewal, fertility, cleansing, marriage, love, balance of opposites, looking deeper and beyond appearances, communication with the spirit world

Essential Oil: Hawthorn berry essential oil is available and is a rich source of polyphenols.

Gemstone: Poppy jasper—courage, strength, will power, heals heartbreak

Magic: The hawthorn is also called the Fairy Tree, the Lonely Bush, and the Queen of May. Fairies are said to curse anyone who harms it. The end of the dark, cold winter nights and the beginning of spring, fertility, and new life were heralded by the blossoming of the hawthorn tree. It is customary to hang strips of rags on the Hawthorn tree during Beltane festivities. It is the tree of enchantment.

Young maidens held twigs of the hawthorn (at Beltane, May 1) for attracting a husband. Bathing in the dew of the hawthorn would bring about beauty for women.

To invoke protection, take nine thorns from the hawthorn tree, wrap them in a piece of fresh linen and write the name of the person or thing you wish protection from. Place on your altar during the month of May and protection will be granted.

Notable Associations: Loki, Sun God Belenus, Jesus, Blodeuwedd, Cardea, Flora, Hera, Hyman

Medicine: Hawthorn tea, tincture, or cordial can help with regulating blood pressure and is a natural sedative. It also makes a nice jelly and has been called "valerian of the heart." It is used in China and India for digestive issues.

Caution: Never use hawthorn without a doctor's consent.

Practical Uses: Hawthorn is frequently used as a rootstock in grafting pear trees. It is a hard wood and resistant to rot; therefore, it is a good raw material to make fence posts and handles.

Conservation: Hawthorn may be prone to aphid attack, gall mites, and the bacterial disease "fire blight."

Hawthorn Tree Magic—Protection Spell with Crystals and Hawthorn

You will need:

- Gemstones: Amethyst, Selenite, Black Tourmaline, Poppy, or Red Jasper (four small stones)
- nine thorns from a Hawthorn tree
- six to eight inch square or round of fresh linen
- A permanent marking pen
- String or ribbon to tie the package

Directions

1. Write the name of the person or thing you request protection from on the linen cloth.

2. Picture that thing or person in your mind as you add the stones and the thorns to the linen piece. With each thing you place in the linen, say, "*I ask for protection from_____*" (Should be repeated twelve times).

3. Gather the ends and tie the linen and contents into a bag. Secure and close the bag with string or ribbon.

4. Tie another loop of ribbon around the bag to hang it.

5. Place the packet near the front door, your bedroom door, or any place that feels right to you.

6. Every time you see the packet, say the word "*Amen*," or whatever phrase you prefer to make it so.

Hazel (*Corylus*)

Hazel (*Corylus*)

The trees range from 10 to 120 feet in height, are part of the birch family (*Betulaceae*), and their nuts are hazelnuts, equally loved by humans, squirrels, and other wildlife. Hazel is one of the most useful trees for its flexible stems and is a conservation savior because it is home to many animals, birds, and insects.

Hazelwood is used for dowsing and burned in the fires at Beltane. It was known as the Tree of Knowledge in Celtic times and was one of the nine sacred trees for the Celts. It was considered bad luck to chop down a hazel tree and was punishable by death. Hazelwood was never burned in homes. It was only used for sacred, ceremonial, community fires.

> A hazel wand protects against evil spirits and is a powerful tool.

Ogham: The letter C—Coll

Symbolism: Wisdom, chastity, spirituality, prophecy, healing

Essential Oil: Hazelnut oil (*Corylus avellana*) is a carrier oil. It has a high concentration of omega-9 and vitamin E and moisturizes, protects, and helps maintain the skin's elasticity and suppleness.

Gemstone: Brown labradorite—spiritual expansion, higher levels of mind

Magic: It is said that if you want your wishes to come true, make a crown of hazelwood leaves, wear them for one hour, and think of the wishes you want granted. Eating hazelnuts will increase your wisdom and bring fertility. A hazel wand protects against evil spirits and is a powerful tool. Carry a hazelnut as a charm, and you will be protected and have visions of the other world. Nine is the number for hazel, so if you drop nine nuts into a bowl of spring water, look deeply into the bowl, and you will be able to see the future.

> Nine is the number for hazel, so if you drop nine nuts into a bowl of spring water, look deeply into the bowl, and you will be able to see the future.

Notable Associations: Mercury, Thor, Artemis, and Diana

Medicine: Hazelnut is an antioxidant and provides vitamins C, E, and D, and copper, manganese, calcium, potassium, and phosphorus minerals. It helps prevent heart disease. Hazelnuts strengthen the immune system and reduce fatigue and tiredness. If you make a tea of hazelnuts, you will attract customers to your business.

Caution: Check for allergic reactions, especially if you are allergic to peanuts.

Practical Uses: Oil extracted from the European filbert, or common hazel (*Corylus avellana*), is used in food products, perfumes, and soaps. The tree yields a reddish-white soft timber, useful for small articles such as tool handles and walking sticks.

Hazel wood can be twisted or knotted and has many uses. These include thatching spars, net stakes, water-divining sticks, hurdles, and furniture.

Conservation: Hazels are conservators of the forest. When coppiced (cut down to ground level), they provide a haven for many birds, insects, lichens, rodents, and wildlife. They also grow stronger and straighter when coppiced and grow back naturally.

How to Use a Wand for Magic

Wands have a variety of uses and are sensitive energy conductors. You can use them for casting spells, healing, enchanting objects, and summoning spirits. You may want to follow a few steps in preparing your wand for magical work.

1. Cleanse your wand using crystals, earth, fir needles, music, sage, cedar chips, moonlight, sunlight, or water.

2. Bring yourself into a centered state. Consecrate your wand for good magic and white lightwork.

3. Charge your wand by rubbing your hands together for thirty seconds and then placing both hands over your wand. Say, "*Behold, I bestow upon you my magical energy for the work we will do together. We are hereby bound together for all eternity. Amen.*" (Or whatever phrase you are comfortable using.)

4. Set your intention for the kind of activity you are about to commence. Say it aloud.

5. Wand etiquette. Hold your wand in your right hand for invoking, summoning, praying, or chanting. Hold the wand in your left hand when banishing or dismissing negative spirits. (If you are left-hand dominant, reverse the positions.)

6. For the magical session, find a comfortable way to hold the wand in your hand or fingers. Use this as your holding position. Visualize the energy coming from your crown and heart chakras, down your arm, and into the wand. When you feel that charge of energy transfer to the wand, you are ready to begin.

7. Spell your intention in the air using the wand as your pen for writing.

8. You can use your wand for spells, incantations, enchanting objects, and other magical activities. Practice the spells you know for love, career, health, money, power, and happiness.

9. You can also use the wand for healing. Point the wand to the physical issue or concern without touching the area, and make circles of motion over the area while reciting a prayer, mantra, or incantation. Allow the energy to transfer from the wand to the person to shower healing energy over the person or animal.

10. Never rush a spell. Allow the outcome to occur in natural time.

11. Conclude by thanking all the entities, participants, universal energy, gods, goddesses, faeries, and nature spirits who partook in this magical session.

12. You can also clear auras, cleanse chakras, create a band of protection around yourself or someone else, and dissolve emotional blockages with your wand. Practice often and sincerely for best results.

13. Keep your wand(s) in a safe and sacred place. Cover it with a purple cloth and put it away from public contact. Recharge before your next magical session.

Hemlock (*Tsuga canadensis*)

Hemlock (*Tsuga canadensis*)

The hemlock tree is a tall pyramidal tree with purplish or reddish-brown bark. It is called the Canadian or Eastern hemlock and can grow to seventy-five feet. It features horizontal, slender, drooping branches with short, blunt leaves emanating from the twigs' woody cushions. Small cones hang from the tips of the branches, and the needles are pleasingly fragrant.

Hemlock must not be confused with poison hemlock (*Conium maculatum* native to Europe and Asia. Poison hemlock is sometimes mistaken for fennel, parsley, Queen Anne's lace, or wild carrot because it is in the carrot family. The entire plant is lethal because it can kill animals and humans if enough is eaten.

Poison hemlock contains the neurotoxin *coniine* that causes the central nervous system to shut down. The Greek philosopher Socrates was given a potion made with poison hemlock after being found guilty of corrupting Athenian youth.

Symbolism: Vulnerability, yin energy, introspection, shelter, inner knowledge, radical transformation.

Essential Oil: Hemlock essential oil is steam distilled from conifer trees and is not related to the poisonous hemlock plant (a member of the parsley family). It supports the breath, chest, and throat for colds, congestion, and sore throats.

Gemstone: Charoite—purifying, selflessness, compassion

Magic: Hemlock has subtle magic with a powerful punch. It can turn a sane person mad or vice versa. Use hemlock branches, needles, and boughs with care. You are working with deep, grounded energy that fuels the fire of change in the universe. Boughs placed over your doorway will attract people of tender hearts and bold stances.

> Transformational hemlock holds subtle magic with a powerful punch. It can turn a sane person mad or vice versa.

Notable Associations: Thor, Medea

Medicine: Eastern hemlock has warming qualities to treat the kidney, liver, lower back, and ligaments. Its freshly sprouted needles are edible. The resin is antiseptic and anti-inflammatory and can be used to heal wounds.

Caution: Eastern hemlock contains tannins. The use of eastern hemlock could produce side effects like stomach problems, damage to the kidney and liver, and an increased cancer risk.

Practical Uses: It was used for fires and helped build the railroads by supplying wood for track ties. The wood is high in tannins and used in leather tanning. It is a soft wood and great for making wands. The bark, when boiled, produces a pinkish dye.

Conservation: In a large area of the eastern US, hemlocks are endangered species. An invasive insect is attacking eastern and Carolina hemlocks, causing the death of many trees.

Hemlock Tree Magic—Radical Transformation Ritual

You will need:

+ Hemlock (twigs, branches, incense, or wood chips)

+ 8–12 fresh rose flowers

+ Burning bowl or cauldron, twelve inches

+ Lighting tool

+ A wooden stick, eight to twelve inches

+ Drumming music

Directions

1. Center yourself.

2. Focus on what you want to transform or how you want to be transformed.

3. Put on the music and begin to dance to the beat. (You may want to use a blindfold so you can connect to the music and dance from the heart without feeling self-conscious. Make sure your space is safe for this.) Dance for three to four minutes.

4. Using your stick, draw a line, or use some method of demarcation representing where you want to go. (You can use a hemlock bough if you wish.)

5. Place the roses on the other side of the line.

6. Hold the stick in your hand and tell it what you want to release.

7. Break the stick and place it in the burning bowl. Add the wood chips or twigs and light them on fire. (Be fire careful.)

8. Burn the hemlock incense.

9. As the bowl burns (safely), cross the line and collect your roses.

10. The transformation has occurred.

---

11. Raise your arms in gratitude for your new life, and take a few minutes to sense the change and allow it to settle in your heart. Smell the roses.

12. Express your gratitude verbally and thank all the energies of nature that brought you here.

Suggestion:

"In deepest gratitude, I say 'thank you' to the generous bounty of nature that allowed me to transform myself and my life today (or whatever you want to be transformed). I take you into my heart forevermore and vow to spread the magic and goodness of this day. Bless you, for giving me your love and support and showing me the beauty of change. I am transformed. Amen." (Or use whatever closing phrase or signature you wish.)

Holly *(Ilex aquifolium)*

Holly *(Ilex aquifolium)*

The holly tree grows to fifty feet tall and bears shining, spiny, dark evergreen leaves and usually red berry fruits. It can also grow as a single-trunk tree or a multi-stemmed thicket. In some parts of the world, holly is sacred; in others, it is considered a weed.

Druids decorated their huts with evergreens and holly during winter as an abode for the sylvan spirits during Alban Arthan, Winter Solstice, and Yule. Western Christmas decorations are derived from customs observed by the Romans whereby they sent boughs and other gifts to their friends during the festival of the Saturnalia. Pliny describes Holly under the name of *Aquifolius*, needle leaf, and adds that it was the same tree called *Crataegus* by Theophrastus (Grieve 2021). The holly tree is a hardwood, and since the leaves remain for three years, it qualifies as an evergreen too.

In olden times, Celtic chieftains donned a holly wreath worn as a crown for good luck. Holly was named for the birth of the holly king and represented the death of the oak king (half the year), while the new king was born to reign until the Summer Solstice. The Druids believed holly brought protection, so they frequently wore holly in their hair.

A Christian holly legend states that the berries had once been white until touched by the blood of Jesus when a holly wreath served as his martyr's crown (Paghat.com 2021).

Ogham: The Letter T—Tinne

Symbolism: Unconditional love, sacrifice, reincarnation, protection against evil, material fortune

Essential Oil: Holly berry essential oil is available. However, the quality and purity of private distillation and extraction cannot be guaranteed. Compatible essential oil is red thyme (*Thymus vulgaris*).

Gemstone: Red jasper—grounding, justice, peace, insight

Magic: A holly wand is good for removing evil spirits and unwanted entities or energies. This tree is about change, moving on, growth, and remembering the past. If it is not used with respect and caution, it can be poisonous. It wards off evil. It has protective and killing aspects.

> A holly wand is good for removing evil spirits, unwanted entities or energies, change, moving on, growth, and remembering the past.

Notable Associations: Lugh, Thor, Freya

Medicine: Holly leaves were dried and made into healing teas. Hot compresses made of holly leaves helped cure broken bones. Holly is not used much these days in alternative medicine. Holly's properties are triterpenes beta amyrin, flavonoids, rutin, quercetin nitrile, glycosides, ilicin, phytosterols, caffeic acid, chlorogenic acid, and traces of theobromine (in the leaves) (The Herbal Resource 2021).

Caution: The berries of the holly tree are poisonous to humans and animals. Do not consume.

Practical Uses: Holly makes a hot fire. The wood is white and retains its resin. Dry well before working with it or staining. If sanded with fine-grit paper, the wood will develop a high luster. Holly makes a wonderful wand in glistening white and is a stunning walking stick.

Conservation: Several holly species are endangered. One holly, *Ilex gardneriana*, is extinct because of habitat loss. It is endemic to the Nilgiri Hills of India.

Jacaranda (*Jacaranda mimosifolia*)

Jacaranda (*Jacaranda mimosifolia*)

In the Guarani language, jacaranda means *fragrant*. There are approximately fifty species of jacaranda.

One of the most vivid memories I have of the jacaranda tree is when I moved to Los Angeles in the late sixties and encountered the massive blooming of the jacaranda trees in the city. Once a year, the lined streets burst into a vibrant purple color, and you could barely see the sun for the arbor of purple blossoms filling the sky. The sight is magnificent, the perfume is intoxicating, and the lawns and sidewalks are covered in purple blossom snow for a month while the trees put on their annual party clothes.

The debt for the spectacular month of purple heaven goes to Katherine Olivia "Kate" Sessions (1857–1940), a horticulturist and botanist who brought the jacarandas to Los Angeles in the early twentieth century. In 1933, jacaranda was declared the most exotic tree in Los Angeles.

The jacaranda tree is exceptionally hardy, drought-resistant, and has few pests or disease issues. It grows fast up to forty feet tall. It prefers a full to partial sun location with plenty of growing room. These elegant trees can live for two hundred years.

> Jacaranda is magnificent, the perfume is intoxicating, and lawns and sidewalks are covered in purple blossom snow for a month while the trees put on their annual party clothes.

Symbolism: Wisdom, rebirth, wealth, and good luck

A famous myth tells of the Daughter of the Moon, who descended from the jacaranda tree and lived among the villagers to share her heaven-sent knowledge, wisdom and ethics, and the difference between good and evil. When she had completed her teachings, she flew back into the heavens.

Essential Oil: Jacaranda essential oil is available and has microbial properties. It has been used for treating bacterial infections, gonorrhea, syphilis, and leukemia.

Gemstone: Purple tourmaline—purification, achievement, affability

Magic: If a jacaranda blossom falls on your head, you will have good luck. Use the bark in spells for healing negative thoughts. Replace them with statements of healing, plenty, and abiding by the golden rule. Use jacaranda blossoms to create a gratitude ritual wherein you state your appreciation for every lesson learned in your life and view all of them as gifts.

> Use jacaranda blossoms to create a gratitude ritual wherein you state your appreciation for every lesson learned in your life and view all of them as gifts.

Notable Associations: Daughter of the Moon

Medicine: Jacaranda has been used to treat bacterial infections, gonorrhea, syphilis, neuralgia, varicose veins, acne, wounds, skin infections, and leukemia. There are several ways to use the tree. Some use essential oils derived from the leaves, others from the bark, seeds, or flowers. Others use a water extract of any of the same parts. The flowers from the jacaranda can be used in the fight against cancer (Surviving Mexico 2019).

Caution: Pregnant or breastfeeding women should not use jacaranda.

Practical Uses: Jacaranda wood is used for cabinetry, furniture, poles, tool handles, and small carvings. The dried wood is also used for fuel in winter.

Conservation: Jacaranda is not listed with either the Convention in International Trade in Endangered Species of Wild Fauna and Flora (CITES) Appendices or the International Union for Conservation of Nature (IUCN) as being threatened or endangered (Removers 2021).

Juniper *(Juniperus)*

Juniper *(Juniperus)*

There is much discussion about the number of juniper species. Some experts say fifty, and others say sixty-seven. No matter the squabbling, some of the most beautiful trees in the world are juniper. You can find them throughout the northern hemisphere, from the Arctic all the way south to tropical Afri and into the mountains of Central America.

Junipers vary in size and shape from tall trees, 65 to 130 feet, to columnal or low spreading with elegant branches.

Some junipers are given the common name "cedar," including *Juniperus virginiana*, the "red cedar" used widely in drawers and closets.

Symbolism: Purification of home, funerary rites, banish evil spirits, curses, protection

Essential Oil: Juniper essential oil is made from juniper berries. Juniper berries are steam-distilled to produce an essential oil that may vary from colorless to yellow or pale green. Its chemical components are alphapinene, cadinene, camphene, and terpineol. It has antiseptic, antimicrobial, antibacterial, and anti-fungal properties.

Gemstone: Green kyanite—high energy channel, attunement, meditation, psychic conductor

Magic: Carry a bowl of smoking juniper needles throughout the home to cleanse the areas, especially the corners where spirits may lurk. Place fresh juniper boughs over the door and windows to protect the home from unwanted entities or spells. Use a dot of juniper oil on used items you purchase to send away unwanted vibrations of the former owner. Once a month, at the new moon, use juniper smudge to clean out your space from anything negative. Cleanse crystals in juniper needles or place in a sand bath.

> Place fresh juniper boughs over the door and windows to protect the home from unwanted entities or spells.

Notable Associations: Hel, Thor, Tyr

Medicine: Cade oil is distilled from juniper wood (*Juniperus oxycedrus*). But juniper oil is made from juniper berries (*Juniperus communis*), which we use for healing. Juniper helps digestion, urinary tract infections, and kidney stones. The Navajo have traditionally used juniper to treat diabetes. Native Americans also used juniper berries as a female contraceptive.

Caution: Do not use juniper essential oil if you are pregnant or breastfeeding. Juniper berries may cause skin irritation or kidney sensitivity.

Practical Uses: In foods, juniper berry is often used as a condiment and flavoring for foods and fragrances in soaps and cosmetics. Juniper wood has a smooth and lovely finish. It is used for making furniture and paneling. Juniper berries are a spice used in a wide variety of culinary dishes and are best known for the primary flavoring in gin (and responsible for gin's name, which is a shortening of the Dutch word for juniper, *genever*). Juniper berries are also used as the primary flavor in the liquor Jenever and the sahti-style of beers. Juniper berry sauce is often a popular flavoring choice for quail, pheasant, veal, rabbit, venison, and other meat dishes (American Conifer Society 2021).

Conservation: The common juniper in the UK is vulnerable to extinction.

Lemon (*Citrus Limon*)

Lemon (*Citrus Limon*)

Citrus trees thrive in the warm, humid temperatures of tropical and subtropical climates. Lemon trees cannot tolerate frost or cold temperatures. People living in colder climates may choose to grow their lemon trees indoors. Meyer lemon, for example, grows well indoors.

There are over twenty different varieties of lemons, from Persian lemons to Baboon lemons from Brazil to Femminello lemons from Italy to Bush lemons from Australia and Buddha's Hand lemons from the Himalayas. Each lemon is unique in its flavor, texture, color, and shape.

One thing common to all lemon trees is that they give a fruit that multiple cultures love around the globe. It is used in medicine, healing, cooking, cleaning, and as an offering to the gods and goddesses of the regions.

If the truth be known, my dream was to move to California when I was fifteen to be able to have lemons and oranges in my backyard. Goal achieved, and I once brought a lemon tree from Guadalajara back home on the plane with me to Los Angeles that grew to be forty feet tall and provided me with the best lemons of my life for over forty years. Yes, I am deeply in love with lemons.

Symbolism: Fertility, uplifting, happiness, joy, cleansing, love, light

Essential Oil: Lemon (*Citrus limon*) essential oil is cold-pressed from the peels of lemon fruit. It has antibacterial, antifungal, astringent, and antimicrobial properties. You can use it for cleaning, healing, emotional lifts, and spiritual practices.

Gemstone: Citrine—creativity, intuition, self-esteem, confidence, abundance, counteracts negativity

Magic: Use lemon peels or lemon essential oil in rituals to cleanse, purify, and to be rid of negative energies or thoughts. For sweet dreams, place some dried lemon leaves under your pillow before you go to sleep.

Notable Associations: Aphrodite, Gaea, Hera, Diana

Medicine: Lemon has antibacterial, antioxidant, vitamin C properties. It may reduce cancer risk, prevent anemia, help with weight loss, improve digestion, prevent kidney stones, calm the mood, elevate the spirit, and is a good wound cleanser. Use the juice of the lemon, lemon essential oil, or lemon peel for your medicinal purposes.

Caution: Lemon is phototoxic and can cause damage to the skin if worn in the sun. Wait twelve hours after applying a lemon product to your skin before going outdoors.

> Lemon is phototoxic and can cause damage to the skin if worn in the sun. Wait twelve hours after applying a lemon product to your skin before going outdoors.

Practical Uses: When citrus wood is dried, it sheds its bark, making it lighter and easier to transport. It burns well for fires and is used in smoking meats and cooking. It is also used in making furniture, hiking sticks, cabinets, and engraver's blocks.

Conservation: *Huanglongbing*, or citrus greening disease, spread by an insect called the Asian citrus psyllid, is threatening California's citrus crop. Up to 12,000 psyllids can accumulate on a single tree during a sixty-day flush period, and a tree can die in under five years. Florida's citrus crop has already been grossly affected. Once there is an infestation, there is no cure.

Making Magical Moon Water with Lemons

In your magical work, you will frequently need water for spells and blessings. Using magical lemon moon water will enhance your magic and increase the potency of your spells. Here's how to make it.

1. On the night of a full moon, pour 1 liter of spring water (or rainwater you have collected) into a glass bowl.

2. Add the juice of half a lemon, 3 lemon peels, and the petals from one live rose and place a moonstone at the bottom of the bowl.

3. Protect the top from outside curious critters with a net or mesh covering.

4. Allow the bowl to remain outside in the moonlight until dawn.

5. In the morning, bring the bowl inside and strain the water into a glass bottle and put a top on it.

6. Label it as "Moon Water for Rituals" and keep it in a cool, dark place, preferably a refrigerator where others won't mistake it for a beverage.

7. Never drink this water and never boil it. Use it for your magic work only.

8. The water is powered by the moon's energy and will enhance and amplify the power of your spells and magical work.

Linden *(Tilia europaca)*

Linden *(Tilia europaca)*

The linden tree, commonly known as basswood or lime tree, is not related to the fruit-bearing bush of the same name but is part of the Tilia genus. Linden trees are known for their stunning foliage, heavy flowering ability, and statuesque form. They also produce delicious honey-nectar. The trees are most commonly found throughout Europe and North America, with some trees in parts of Asia. Lindens are large trees and usually planted as street trees, in parks, and in large places. Once pollinated, the flowers develop oval, slightly ribbed fruits with a pointed tip. The linden blossom aroma is complex with overtones of spice and honey.

Linden trees are perfectly balanced, they are hermaphroditic, meaning their flowers carry both the male and female parts that require insects for pollination.

Symbolism: Tranquility, love, longevity, prophecy

Essential Oil: Linden blossom essential oil is used in perfumes for its scent. It has been used to induce sweating for alleviating feverish colds and infections and reducing nasal congestion, sore throat, and cough.

Gemstone: Yellow calcite—self-confidence, hope, clearing old patterns

Magic: Use linden flowers for love spells; add them to your incense. Dried linden flowers mixed with lavender and lemon blossoms placed in a sachet will induce sleep. Use dried linden leaves for purification when made into a smudge stick or used in a bowl. Live, fresh linden flowers placed in a room will keep all spirits healthy and vibrant. If you dream of a linden tree, your marriage or love relationship is in grave danger. Use linden oil for making prophecies and connecting with the seer inside.

> Dried linden flowers mixed with lavender and lemon blossoms placed in a sachet will induce sleep.

Notable Associations: Freya, Frigg, Venus

Medicine: Linden tea has been used for mild pain, to induce relaxation, reduce inflammation, and as a mild diuretic. It can soothe digestion, lower blood pressure, and induce sleep. Linden essential oil can help anxiety because it is a nervine, antispasmodic, and can ease spasms and cramps associated with headaches, tight muscles, and migraines.

Caution: Do not use during pregnancy or while breastfeeding or taking medications to reduce blood pressure.

Practical Uses: The fine grain of the linden wood makes beautiful furniture and has been used for making guitars, drum casings, and fine wood carvings, some of which can be viewed in Windsor Castle.

Conservation: The linden tree is not on the endangered list.

Tree Magic—Cutting the Cords

Ongoing relationships, past traumas, some persons, places, or things can evoke a maelstrom of emotion in us. These are cords that bind us to the past. When that cord pulls energy from you or drains you, you may want to consider cutting it like a tree that needs seasonal pruning to grow tall, straight, and strong.

Our internal energy systems, like those of trees, are continuously sending and receiving energy from our environment and the people around us. If a past relationship still has us emotionally caught, we may not move forward. It's time to cut that cord.

Cutting cords frees us from emotional entanglements that prevent a healthier relationship. Like the tree, we need to prune the limbs and suckers that sap our energy.

How to Cut a Cord:

1. Place yourself in a meditative, relaxed state and breathe.

2. Focus on an object and let go of all mental chatter and distracting thoughts.

3. Bring into your mind the person, place, thing, or incident that causes you emotional pain.

4. Picture a visible cord between you (your body) and the person, place, or incident.

5. Hold your hand like it is a pair of scissors. (Remember how you played Rock, Paper, Scissors as a kid.) Or, if you prefer, emulate a karate chop movement with the side of your hand.

6. Bring the person, place, or incident into clear focus. Picture the cord that connects you. Then, in one swift motion, cut or chop the visible cord with your hand and watch them float away into the sky until you can no longer see them.

7. Visualize the cord attached to your body melting and dissolving into nothing.

8. Revel in this moment of self-initiated freedom. You are no longer emotionally connected by this cord, and you are free.

9. Open your eyes and raise your arms skyward in gratitude for the release from the bonds that have held you. Express your thanks.

Mahogany Tree (Swietenia mahagoni)

Mahogany Tree (*Swietenia mahagoni*)

The mahogany tree can reach fifty to two hundred feet in height and six feet in diameter. Its name means *rich, dark wood*. The trees grow in hot climates like South Florida, the Bahamas, Honduras, Borneo, and the Caribbean. Bees love the flowers and make excellent honey from the blossoms.

In nature they are used as shade and ornamental trees. They are statuesque trees that stand tall and strong. Their majesty commands respect and can withstand lightning strikes; hence they are deemed magical.

The tree is prized for its hardwood and makes unique, rare, and exquisite furniture.

Symbolism: Strength, safety, protection, magic

Essential Oil: Mahogany oil (*Swietenia mahagoni*) is used in wood-staining and beard-grooming. It also comes as a fragrance oil. However, the quality and purity of private distillation and extraction cannot be guaranteed.

Gemstone: Polished stromatolite—transformation, dissolves blockages, healing

Magic: A mahogany wand is a rare find and treat. Because mahogany is a luxurious hardwood prized for its straight grain and mesmerizing reddish-brown color. The wood conducts vibration well, so many fine musical instruments are made from it. It has a deep, warm, energetic vibration. Use your mahogany wand to create safety, protection, strength and know that this is its natural magic.

Notable Associations: Shango, Zeus, Nzazi

Medicine: Tea made from mahogany bark and seeds can reduce fever and the effects of diarrhea. It has traditionally been used for toothache and chest pains and improves blood circulation and lowers high cholesterol. This remedy also claims to improve men's sexual vitality.

Borneo mahogany oil is harvested from the nut kernel of the Borneo mahogany tree and is good for acne, aging skin, blemishes, and athlete's foot. It is antibacterial, antiseptic, antifungal, antiviral, and anti-inflammatory.

Caution: Test skin for allergic reaction before applying.

Practical Uses: The trees are raised for their hard, durable wood and used to make cabinets and furniture. Mahogany is frequently used in the tops of guitars and the back, sides, and necks of instruments of the mandolin and guitar families. Mahogany is unlikely to warp, shrink, or swell. It is also resistant to rot.

Conservation: The species is becoming increasingly rare and has been added to Florida's endangered species list. Be cautious of your source before purchasing, and make sure it comes from sustainable growers.

Magnolia (*Magnolia grandiflora*)

Magnolia (*Magnolia grandiflora*)

There are eighty different species of the magnolia tree. It is also known as *Champa*. The *champaca* tree is a magnolia with highly prized golden blossoms. Magnolia essential oil is fragrant and affordable, whereas *champaca* essential oil is triple the price and amazingly fragrant.

The magnolia can grow up to sixty feet tall. It is unique because it has a single taproot instead of many. They can live 120 years. Another unique thing about the flowering magnolia tree is that its blossoms are only ready for fertilization by the beetles for a day or two. After that, the season closes.

The flowers come in colors like green, pink, purple, white, and yellow. Magnolias are ancient plants. They existed on Earth ninety-six million years ago and have, over time, adapted their flowers to become attractive to beetles since beetles are now their only pollinator and the key to their propagation.

Magnolia trees are generally resistant to pests, having evolved for over ninety-six million years. It is said that Venus bestowed the beautiful fragrance on the magnolia tree. In China, magnolias were the perfect symbols of feminine beauty and gentle nature.

Every day, I walk my dogs through a grove of magnolia trees. We always come back from the walk feeling transformed physically from the exercise and lifted by the emotions of calm, peace, and tranquility that these gorgeous trees provide. When they are in full bloom in the summertime, it is positively intoxicating to stroll among them.

Symbolism: Adaptability, healing, love, loyalty, restoration

Essentials Oils: Magnolia oil is steam-distilled from the sturdy petals of the magnolia flower. Like lavender and bergamot, magnolia is primarily linalool, which may help with feelings of stress or anxiousness and can be relaxing.

Gemstone: Scolecite—intuition, inner vision, inner peace, transformation, enlightenment

Magic: Magnolia twigs or chips have been used for healing spells. Wear a magnolia amulet for control of anxiety. To attract good fortune, hang magnolia seed pods over your doorways and windows. Cast spells using magnolia to increase passion, awaken loyalty, summon luck, attract lasting love, and create emotional balance.

> Magnolia twigs or chips have been used in healing spells. Wear a magnolia amulet to control anxiety. Hang magnolia seed pods over your doorways and windows to bring good fortune.

Notable Associations: Venus, Aphrodite, Narasimha, Vishnu

Medicine: The magnolia tree makes *magnolol*, which has been beneficial in treating leukemia and colon cancer in the early trial stages. The bark of *Magnolia oficinalis* has been used in traditional Chinese medicine for centuries to help relieve anxiety, tension, and insomnia. It is believed that *honokiol*, a chemical property in magnolia bark, is responsible for the effects. Their properties are anti-inflammatory, antimicrobial, and antioxidant. Use magnolia essential oil diluted in a carrier oil for sore muscles, scrapes, and to soothe minor burns.

Caution: Magnolia can make you sleepy, so do not use if taking sedatives.

Practical Uses: Magnolia wood is used for pallets and furniture like cabinets and shelving. It is also used in wooden bowls and utensils.

Conservation: The latest Red List to be published under the Global Tree Assessment shows that half of all *Magnolia* species are threatened with extinction in the wild. To find such a high proportion of threatened species in such a well-known and widely cultivated plant family is alarming and signals the need for more concerted conservation action to protect these valuable trees (Murphy 2016).

Maple (*Acer*)

Maple (*Acer*)

The common maple sports 128 different species, from the sugar maple to the black maple to the Japanese maple and beyond. The maple tree will grow pretty much anywhere if you know how to care for it. The maple tree is deciduous and loses its leaves in the fall. The maple leaf is distinct in shape and easily recognized. The sugar maple is the national tree of Canada and the name of a Canadian hockey team.

The sugar maple is prized for its sap, and we've all certainly experienced a scrumptious pancake breakfast with golden maple syrup flowing across and down the fluffy stack. Deciduous trees produce sap, while non-deciduous trees like conifers produce resin.

Sugar maple, *Acer pseudoplatanus*, is the most common maple species in Europe. It is known as the sycamore and goes back one hundred million years. These amazing trees can easily live to be six hundred years old. This sycamore reference is not to be confused with the sycamore in ancient Egyptian times because that was the sycamore fig.

They have offered their generous shade for millennia and will continue to do so if there is oxygen to breathe and water to feed them.

Symbolism: Development, perseverance, vitality, humility, harmony

Essential Oil: Maple essential oil is available, as is maple-pecan, maple-teak, and more. However, the quality and purity of private distillation and extraction cannot be guaranteed. Compatible essential oil is sandalwood (*Santalum album*).

Gemstone: Red sardonyx—purification, protection, bravery, perception

Magic: Excellent in spells for prosperity, success, or love. Use maple leaves or sap as the medium. Work with ancestors and spells to summon their help. Create energy with maple/sycamore and learn the lesson of humility. Maple is the wood of the traveler and makes a great wand. If you want to enhance intellectual pursuits, acquire new knowledge, or excel at communication, maple is your wood. Gypsies believe maple brings gold and that eating the seeds draws in love.

Notable Associations: Bran, Danu, Dagda, Jupiter, Zeus, Rhea

Medicine: Like honey, maple sap can traditionally fight infections in wounds. The medicinal properties of the maple leaf are sedative and tonic. It is an excellent remedy for the liver and spleen. It is a reviving tonic. Use the power or bark as an infusion for tea. Sap from various maple trees has been shown to support osteoporosis, prevent gastric ulcer formation, lower blood pressure, mitigate alcoholic hangovers, support a healthy immune system, and offer dietary antioxidants (Haritan 2021).

Caution: It is advised to boil natural tree sap before ingesting in case of bacteria.

Practical Uses: Maple wood is frequently used in furniture, flooring, cabinetry, and kitchen accessories. Because it is durable and strong, maple can be used as flooring in bowling alleys and for bowling pins.

Conservation: The maple tree is not endangered.

Maple Tree Magic—Prosperity Ritual or Spell

You will need:

- A green stone like aventurine or red sardonyx
- Silver or gold coins (i.e., new pennies/nickels/quarters/dimes/silver dollars or feng shui Chinese coins)
- Lodestone magnetic sand in silver or gold (available online)
- Money-drawing potion (mix 3 teaspoons ground maple leaves together with 3 teaspoons sugar)
- A small purple bowl

Directions

1. Place the coins in the bowl.

2. Place the stones on top of the coins.

3. Sprinkle a third of the money-drawing potion and 4 tablespoons of the magnetic sand over the coins and the stones.

4. Place the bowl under your bed and ensure no pets or children can get into the bowl. Say: *"Prosperity finds me and blesses me with its bounty, this day and every day, Amen."* (Or however you close a prayer or affirmation.)

5. Every 3 days, for a total of 3 times, sprinkle the bowl with another third of the money drawing potion and 1 more tablespoon of magnetic sand.

6. Each night before going to sleep, hold the bowl in your hands and visualize how prosperity will find you, how you feel when you have it, and exactly what you can do to attract it. Be specific. ("I will do x, y, and z to bring prosperity into my life.") Hold this thought in your mind as you place the bowl back under your bed and go to sleep.

7. After nine days, accept that the prosperity spell is complete. Return the ingredients to the earth (you may keep the stone and coins with you) and know that prosperity is yours.

8. Make a list of all the things you already have that make you feel prosperous. Bless them and leave the list under the stone and coins. Read the list daily.

Mulberry (*Morus*)

Mulberry (*Morus*)

Besides being mentioned in a nursery rhyme ("Here we go 'round the mulberry bush"), mulberry is a tree with many interesting aspects. It can grow to sixty feet, and it prefers growing in moist forests near streams. Mulberry is part of the fig family, and there are sixteen varieties of mulberry. Mulberries fruit after ten years and have black, purple, pink, red, or white flowers.

The white mulberry tree serves as the food for the silkworm and a place for them to cocoon.

The artist Vincent Van Gogh immortalized the mulberry tree in a few of his paintings. Legend tells that Alexander the Great drank mulberry juice to acquire strength for conquering Persia and India.

Symbolism: Balance, defense, bravery, wisdom

In China, mulberry is the symbol of yin and yang.

Essential Oil: Mulberry essential oil is primarily used as a fragrance oil. Any other mulberry oil cannot be guaranteed for quality and purity due to private distillation and extraction. Comparable essential oil is tangerine (*Citrus Reticulata*).

Gemstone: Dark Sugalite—finding purpose, physical healing, protection

Magic: Mulberry leaves can be used in charm bags to give strength in difficult situations. Use in all workings for protection. Steep a handful of leaves in 1

cup water and add this infusion to your bath or floor washes for purification and courage. Mulberry leaves can also be burned to create smoke to ward off evil spirits from a person, place, or thing.

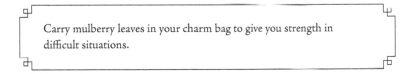

Carry mulberry leaves in your charm bag to give you strength in difficult situations.

Notable Associations: Athena, Minerva

Medicine: Mulberries contain vitamins C, A, E, and K and minerals such as potassium, iron, and magnesium. Mulberries have significantly high amounts of phenolic flavonoid phytochemicals called anthocyanins. Scientific studies have shown that the consumption of mulberries has potential health effects against cancer, aging and neurological diseases, inflammation, diabetes, and bacterial infections.

Ancient Romans were said to have used leaves of the white mulberry for treating diseases of the mouth, trachea, and lungs.

Native Americans used mulberry as a laxative and as a cure for dysentery. The berries contain resveratrol, another polyphenol flavonoid antioxidant.

Caution: Black mulberry could lower blood sugar in diabetics.

Practical Uses: The lightweight mulberry wood is good for making fence posts and barrels. Mulberry branches make glorious baskets. Mulberries are famous for being turned into wine, fruit juice, and jam. They can also be dried and consumed as a healthy snack.

Mulberries can be added to salads. They are great for jams, jellies, cookies, and desserts. They can also be used in smoothies and as a topping for yogurt or ice cream.

Conservation: The red mulberry has been assessed as being endangered.

Myrtle (*Myrtus*)

Myrtle (*Myrtus*)

The myrtle tree is sacred to Aphrodite. Many myrtle trees were planted around Aphrodite's temple gardens and shrines. You may see her depicted with a myrtle crown, sprig, or wreath in her hair.

Myrtle produces blooms in pink, purple, and even red hues. It is a delicate-looking tree, elegant and captivating. One of the nicest things about the myrtle tree is that it blooms mid-summer throughout fall, keeping the burst of color as eye candy for the spectator.

Myrtle requires a mild climate and delicate fertilization and is best when given proper attention.

In mythology, Athena changed Myrsìne, a young girl, into a myrtle bush because she dared to win over a male competitor in the games. In fact, the victory crowns for the winners were made from myrtle leaves. In a sense, Athena did Myrsìne a favor because she would be looked up to and forever on the heads of the winning athletes of the Olympic Games. Also, in ancient Greece, myrtle was used during funeral rites as an homage to the deceased. Myrtle berries were turned into ink and used as a black, indelible dye for fabric.

A lovely tradition in England began with Queen Victoria in 1840 when she married Albert. Her bouquet had myrtle sprigs because they represented love. After the wedding, the story goes, Victoria planted the myrtle sprig from her bouquet in her garden on the Isle of Wight. British royal brides since then have carried a bouquet containing a sprig plucked from the same shrub.

Symbolism: Love, longevity, strength, stability, enterprise

Essential Oil: Myrtle essential oil is distilled from the branch of the myrtle tree. It has a sweet, herbal, camphor-like aroma to open the breath and clear the head.

Gemstone: White jade—composure, calm, centering

Magic: A classic spell: Gently collect a myrtle blossom. Combine it in a piece of square muslin with a white jade stone, nine evergreen needles, a naturally shed cat's whisker, and three drops of tea tree oil. Hold it in your palm and allow sunlight to warm it for fifteen to twenty minutes. Bury this parcel under a pathway you frequently cross. You will have a long and happy life and a stable relationship.

Planting a crepe myrtle tree in your yard will keep your relationship strong. This hardy wood makes an excellent wand.

Spell for a Long and Stable Relationship

Collect a myrtle blossom. Combine a white jade stone, nine evergreen needles, a naturally shed cat's whisker, and three drops of tea tree oil in a square piece of muslin. Hold it in your palm and allow sunlight to warm it for fifteen to twenty minutes, then bury this parcel under a pathway you frequently cross. You will have a long and happy life and a stable relationship.

Notable Associations: Venus, Artemis, Aphrodite, Hathor, Astarte, Ashtoreth, Marian, Myrsine, Esther (Hadassah)

Medicine: Myrtle may help reduce inflammation, lung infections, whooping cough, bladder conditions, diarrhea, heartburn, yeast infections, and worms.

A paste of the flowers can be applied externally to cuts and wounds. The root is astringent, detoxicant, and diuretic. Myrtle may help overcome fungus and bacteria.

Caution: Myrtle is not safe to use if you are pregnant or breastfeeding. It is also unsafe for children and may cause breathing problems if used for children under sixteen.

Practical Uses: The most important product from myrtle is *mirto*, a liqueur mainly made from fresh myrtle berries infused with alcohol, water, and sugar or honey. Recipes are jealously guarded, having been handed down by word of mouth in Sardinian and Corsican communities for many centuries. Furniture made from myrtle wood is handsome.

Conservation: The Angle-Stemmed Myrtle from Australia is on the endangered list. Much of the dry rainforest where Angle-Stemmed Myrtle grows has been cleared for urban and rural development and the land trampled by cattle and sheep. Due to the yearly over-harvesting of myrtle branches in the weeks before Sukkot, the wild myrtle is in danger of extinction and has been placed on Israel's Red List of endangered plant species.

Chapter Nine

Magical Trees N–Y

Magical Trees

N–Y

- Neem
- Oak
- Olive

- Orange
- Palm
- Pine

- Redwood
- Rowan
- Sassafras

- Willow
- Yew

Neem Tree (*Azadirachta indica*)

Neem Tree (*Azadirachta indica*)

The neem tree, a member of the mahogany family, is a fast-growing tree referred to as "Nimtree" or "Indian lilac." It grows fifty to a hundred feet tall and has small, fragrant blossoms. The fruit is a drupe, which looks like an olive. Neem is native to Asia and is mostly found in India, Bangladesh, Pakistan, and Burma. The neem tree cannot withstand freezing temperatures but grows well in rocky or sandy soil.

The tree has been worshipped and respected over the centuries because it is said to cure a thousand diseases. Aficionados claim it has a cure for everything.

Neem is still worshipped as a holy tree for rural Indians in south-central India. Neem in the Telugu language is called the *Vepa* or purifier of air. The mere presence of the neem tree near human dwellings is believed to improve human health, acting as a prophylactic against malarial fever and cholera (Wonders of Neem 2021).

> The mere presence of the neem tree near human dwellings is believed to improve human health, acting as a prophylactic against malarial fever and cholera.

Symbolism: Purification, universal healing, protection

Essential Oil: Neem essential oil is a healing oil. It is also used for gardening as an insect repellant and carrier oil. Neem oil is rich in fatty acids, palmitic, linoleic, and oleic acids, which help support healthy skin. It is antiviral, antifungal, antibacterial, and can kill pathogenic bacteria and intestinal worms.

Gemstone: Apple green jasper—internal harmony, positivity, balancing

Magic: Neem leaves are used throughout India for curative and medicinal purposes. Wounds and sores are bound in Neem leaves and the leaves are used to drive away the evil spirit of death which accompanies the mourners during the post-death rituals. After the cremation of the corpse, members of the funeral procession chew the neem leaves sprinkled with water.

On the Hindu New Year's Day, it is essential that every Hindu worship the neem tree and eat its leaves mixed with pepper and sugar. This protects the person from suffering from sickness or disease during the coming year.

Neem leaves work in spells for warding off unwanted illness, evil spirits, and can be burned to purify a home or space and used as a welcome for a newborn. Hang neem leaves on the door of the baby's room.

Notable Associations: Sun

Medicine: Neem tree bark, leaves, and oil are known as universal healers because they can help many diseases. Neem is called the "village pharmacy" in rural India. Neem tree leaves, bark, and oil have been used to treat various ailments from ancient to modern times. Neem plant products have long been used in Ayurvedic and folk medicine, cosmetics, and organic farming pest and disease control.

The physician (Vaidya) believed neem products to have antifungal, anthelmintic, antibacterial, antiviral, diabetic, sedative, and contraceptive properties, which were used for hair growth, immune system boosting, skin-related problems, and more.

Caution: Consuming neem oil or bark can lead to miscarriage.

Practical Uses: As a fungicide, neem oil can control rust, black spots, mildew, scabs, anthracnose, and a blight on plants and flowers. It is the perfect helper for organic farmers. To remove dark circles around your eyes, use a teaspoon of chilled neem paste. Apply externally to your eyelids and place a cucumber peel on each eye for cooling. Wait ten minutes and remove.[2]

Conservation: One scientific group says: "If neem lives up to its early promise it will help to control many of the world's pests and diseases, as well as reduce erosion, desertification, deforestation, and perhaps even slow the rate of increase in population" (The National Academies Sciences Engineering Medicine 1992).

Neem is not endangered and should be propagated more frequently worldwide.

---

2 www.wikihow.com/Make-Fresh-Neem-Leaves-Paste

Oak *(Quercus)*

Oak *(Quercus)*

There are at least five hundred species of oak. Every country or region seems to have an oak with a specialized name. Famous for acorns, the oak is also renowned as a food source for almost every creature in the forest, like squirrels, mice, rats, deer, pigs, bears, and a host of birds from woodpeckers to ducks and pigeons.

An oak can live a thousand years or more and grow to 150 feet high. When it turns a millennium, it begins to slow down and stops producing acorns. Until then, it has produced enough acorns for a thousand forests. Because it was so huge, strong, and prolific, ancients thought it to be *The Tree of Life.*

Truffles grow where oak trees live. Truffle farmers do not plant truffles; instead, they plant oak trees, hoping to create favorable conditions that might invite truffle growth (The Fact Site, Oak Tree Facts 2021).

The prophetess Sibilla announced her prophecies while standing under a sacred oak. The Druids and Germanic tribes of the Celts practiced their nature worship ceremonies in the middle of oak groves. They would not worship without an oak present. The oldest sanctuary of the god Zeus was an oak tree with a spring at its foot. The Romans considered the oak tree to be the property of Jupiter. The temple of Baal, preserved in Damascus, was built in an oak grove. A sacred oak surrounded Abel's tomb. Thanks to its enormous size and great longevity, the oak in the mythology of many of the world's peoples, was the center, the source and that which everything and everyone revolved around.

It was the symbol of fertility and solid protection, primordial strength, and the ability to survive even in the most difficult periods,

> The towering oak is one of the most hallowed trees in the world due to its qualities of strength, authority, endurance, wisdom, and knowledge.

Ogham: The letter D—Duir

Symbolism: Strength, authority, cosmic knowledge, renewal, durability, balancing, fertility, money, healing

Essential Oil: The closest you'll get to oak essential oil is oak moss essential oil. Oakmoss oil is a solvent extracted from the lichen that grows on oak trees. It has a green, woody, slightly fruity, earthy scent.

Gemstone: Carnelian—courage, endurance, energy, leadership, motivation

Magic: The voice of Jupiter rustles in the oak leaves. Plant acorns at the Dark Moon to attract prosperity. Carry acorns in a pouch to send out romantic attractors.

Notable Associations: Brighid, Diana, Athena, Bloduwedd, Mars, Thor, Tyr, Zeus, Jesus

Medicine: If you catch a falling oak leaf, it is believed you will not be sick for the winter. If a sick person is in your house, light a fire of oak wood to draw out the illness and send it upward. If you dream of resting under an oak tree, you will have a long life and prosperity.

Use oak bark for medicinal purposes. It contains strong astringent properties. Internally, taken as tea, it helps fight diarrhea and dysentery. Externally it can help reduce hemorrhoids, inflamed gums, wounds, and eczema. The tannins found in oak can help reduce minor blistering by boiling a piece of the bark in a small amount of water until a strong solution is reached and then applying it to the affected area (The Goddess Tree, Oak 2021).

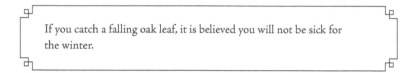

If you catch a falling oak leaf, it is believed you will not be sick for the winter.

Caution: The tannic acid in acorns is poisonous to horses and domestic pets. Oak bark can have serious side effects, including stomach and intestinal symptoms and kidney or liver damage for humans. Do not take oak bark if you are pregnant or breastfeeding or have cardio, kidney, liver, or skin conditions.

Practical Uses: Oak is one of the crucial sources of raw material in our modern times. From the wood of the oak tree, we make elegant furniture, flooring materials, cosmetic creams, and wine barrels, to name a few of the many products produced from oak trees. Vikings built their ships from oak, as did many other seafaring nations needing sturdy vessels.

Conservation: According to a UC Davis plant scientist, a swimming, two-tailed fungus with an appetite for oak bark is probably to blame for the death of thousands of trees in coastal California. The deadly microbe could easily spread to the nation's other oak forests.

Currently, about seventy-eight species of oaks are in danger of extinction. Sadly, farmers in Mexico and Central America are clearing out the oak trees to open grazing land for their cattle and coffee plantations. They use chopped oaks as construction material, and the rest is processed to manufacture the coal (The Fact Site, Oak Tree Facts 2021).

Olive *(Olea europaea)*

Olive *(Olea europaea)*

The Greeks were the first civilization to cultivate and grow olive trees seven thousand years ago. The lifespan of the olive tree is between three and six hundred years if tended well. The Olive Tree of Vouves, on the island of Crete, is the oldest living tree, estimated to be over three thousand years old.

It is believed that the goddess Athena planted an olive tree on the hill of the Acropolis. The tree then became sacred to the Greeks and the official tree of Athens/Athena. Olive branches were used to make crowns and victory wreaths for competing athletes. They were traditionally made of wild-olive leaves from a sacred tree near the temple of Zeus at Olympia. The olive tree holds the record for being sung to the most and praised by the Greeks for millennia—no wonder the olive tree is deeply rooted in Greek mythology, tradition, and history.

There are over 156 million olive trees planted in Greece and only eleven million residents, or a ratio of fourteen to one. Naturally, olive oil is a huge export for the Greeks, weighing 341 thousand tons (Olivida Blog 2021).

The olive tree produces an extremely hard wood resistant to fire and can grow to forty feet tall.

Kew's Herbarium in the UK boasts a wreath of olive leaves believed to be over three thousand years old and was found in the tomb of King Tutankhamun.

For the Celts, the olive tree was the tree of balance; hence it was the official tree of the Autumnal Equinox.

Symbolism: Peace, wisdom, fertility, prosperity, health, victory, stability, fidelity

Essential Oil: Olive oil can be used as a skin emollient and acne preventative and softening and anti-aging. It is a carrier oil as well.

Gemstone: Fluorite—intuition, connection to the spirit, harmonizing

Magic: Carry an olive leaf to bring success and prosperity. Dream of an olive tree, and you will have happiness. Plant an olive tree, and you will get married. Write Athena's name on an olive leaf to attract your mate and place it under your pillow at night. Use olive oil for sacred anointing. Hang a branch over your doorway to attract peace to the house. Smudge a home with olive leaves to create peace and balance of power within. Hang a bare branch of olive wood over each window and doorway to protect from fire. Use the parts of the olive tree to balance the earth energies within yourself.

> Olivelore: Carry an olive leaf to bring success and prosperity. Dream of an olive tree, and you will have happiness. Plant an olive tree, and you will get married.

Notable Associations: Athena, Apollo, Minerva, Ra, Pele, Zeus, Horus, Hercules

Medicine: It is said the tea from the leaves of the olive tree is healing and beneficial for hypertension, cardiovascular disease, diabetes, and hyperlipidemia. Olive oil is loaded with antioxidants, which are biologically active and can reduce the risk of chronic diseases. It is also anti-inflammatory and a monosaturated fat.

Caution: If you are pregnant or breastfeeding check with your doctor before consuming olive leaf tea.

Practical Uses: Olive wood is used in making furniture, kitchen utensils, carvings, wooden bowls decorative carvings.

Conservation: Olive trees are not endangered.

Orange *(Citrus X sinensis)*

Orange *(Citrus X sinensis)*

Who doesn't love an orange, right? Do you wonder if the color came from the tree or if the tree was named for the color? It all originated with the Persian word *narang*, which evolved into *naranja*, and in French became *orange*, and finally in English, *orange*. Today it equally means the fruit and the color.

There are six hundred varieties of the loveable orange around the globe. The fruits of the orange tree are also called oranges, which are nature-modified berries (Spengler 2021).

Oranges are believed to have originated in Southwest China and Northeast India as early as 2500 BCE. For millennia, these bitter-tasting oranges were used mainly for their scent rather than their devouring qualities.

The clever Romans brought the fruit into Europe and Spain in the eighth and ninth centuries. The orange we are most familiar with today was likely developed somewhat later, once the trees hit the sweet sun rays of the Mediterranean climate and soaked up that intense sunshine.

Columbus brought the fruit to America in 1493, and soon afterward, the Portuguese took a few trees to Brazil. Sweet oranges were imported from Portugal by the wealthy Britons in the late sixteenth century.

Oranges are now a prolific crop in warm climates around the world, most notably in Brazil, USA, Spain, North and South Africa, Israel, and Australia.

You will find oranges and mandarin oranges placed on the altars and shrines of Buddhist followers. They are also given as presents during Chinese New Year.

One outstanding member of the family, the amazing Bitter Orange tree— *Citrus aurantium* var. *amara*—produces three different essential oils. The fruit's peel gives us bitter orange essential oil; the flowers produce Neroli essential oil, and the leaves and twigs give us Petitgrain (bigarade) essential oil. ("Bigarade" means it originates from the bitter orange tree.) Definitely a most prolific and generous tree.

Symbolism: Generosity, wisdom, honor

In the Middle Ages, the orange tree represented chastity and purity because maiden brides were required to wear orange flowers in their hair, signifying purity.

Essential Oil: Orange essential oil can be used to lift moods, reduce stress, and as a room freshener. It is antimicrobial, an analgesic, and combats anxiety.

Gemstone: Orange calcite—higher consciousness, clears negativity, aids spiritual growth

Magic: Dried, round, orange slices can be used as altar decorations and in magical spells. Orange peels can fill any spell with wisdom. Use orange powder for prosperity spells. Place a sachet filled with dried orange peels under your pillow to incite prophetic dreams. Add orange peels along with sweet orange essential oil (using a dispersant) to your bath to attract love and friendship. Carry a sachet of orange peels with you when making any business deal for success.

Place a sachet filled with dried orange peels under your pillow to incite prophetic dreams.

Notable Associations: Hesperides, Zeus, Kuan Yin

Medicine: Oranges are good sources of vitamins and minerals. One medium-sized orange has sixty calories, no fat or sodium, twelve grams of natural sugar, one gram of protein, fourteen micrograms of vitamin A, seventy milligrams of vitamin C, and 6 percent of our daily recommended amount of calcium.

One orange gives you all the vitamin C you need in a day.

Caution: If you are taking beta-blockers, avoid oranges. Too many can lower your potassium and damage the kidneys. Oranges are high in acid and can make GERD worse. Too many oranges can cause nausea, vomiting, stomach cramps, headache, and insomnia.

Practical Uses: Orange wood has a yellowy cast and is used in inlaid work for the color and fine woodturning. Dry wood termites can attack the wood. Osage oranges were used for wagon wheels back in the day.

Conservation: The Florida orange is endangered today. An incurable disease called "citrus greening" has swept through the state, affecting every orange-producing county. The disease, called Yellow Dragon in China, is a bacterium spread by a tiny flying insect called a psyllid, which showed up in 2005. Infected trees bear oranges that grow misshapen and bitter. Sadly, the affected trees eventually expire.

Palm *(Arecaceae)*

Palm *(Arecaceae)*

There are over 2,500 species of palm. Some palms can reach up to two hundred feet. Archaeologists have discovered date palms went back to Mesopotamian society five thousand years ago. But, in the true definition of a palm tree, it can mean any of the tropical tree species with long, straight trunks and large frond-like leaves at the top.

Stone carvings read that the Assyrians believed the ultimate symbol of eternity was a palm tree growing beside a stream.

In the Qabalah, the palm tree is an icon for Judea and those who followed Moses out of Egypt.

At the beginning of the modern era, in the time of Christ, people cut palms from trees and laid them in the path of the Messiah as he entered Jerusalem. It is believed that Franciscan missionaries brought palms to California, now a symbol for Hollywood production and films.

The cabbage palm is Florida's state tree.

Some palms have edible fruit, like the coconut palm (*Cocos nucifera*), date palm (*Phoenix dactylifera*), acai from the acai palm (*Euterpe oleracea*), and betel nuts from the Areca (*Areca catechu*) palm. Betel nuts are one of the most popular psychoactive substances in the world, coming in fourth behind nicotine, alcohol, and caffeine. Palm oil is extracted from the *Elaeis guineensis* tree and the seed found in the center of the fruit.

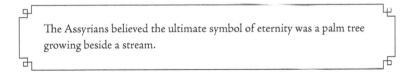

The Assyrians believed the ultimate symbol of eternity was a palm tree growing beside a stream.

Symbolism: Victory, triumph, peace, eternal life, resurrection, male strength

The Palm tree is a solar symbol (masculine) but gives fruit (feminine), so it is gender balanced.

Essential Oil: Red palm oil is vibrant in reddish-orange color packed with carotene and vitamins A and E. It is used as a hair and skin moisturizer. Care should be taken because the color may stain clothing.

Gemstone: Rhyolite—change, variety, progress, balance

Magic: Dry a few dates and use them as talismans for fertility. Dates can also be used as an aphrodisiac. Weave palm fronds into basket bowls for holding your sacred tools and offerings. Weave a bracelet from palm fronds and wear it to achieve invulnerability, health, and protection. Use coconut shells as sacrificial bowls for rituals or ceremonies. Lightly spray plants with a coconut milk mist to remedy poor growth.

Weave palm fronds into basket bowls for holding your sacred tools and offerings. Use coconut shells as sacrificial bowls for ceremonies.

Notable Associations: Apollo, Nike, Jesus, Panaiveriyamman, Cherubim, Sun, Ra, Hathor (date palm) Hel, Thoth and Seshat, Osiris

Medicine: Throughout history, palm tree leaves, seeds, fruit, roots, and bark have been utilized as natural medicine. The fruit from this tree has been used to treat sore throats, colds, bronchial catarrh, fevers, gonorrhea, edema, and abdominal problems. The seeds from the tree have been ground into a paste that effectively treats ague. Date palm roots have relieved toothaches. Finally, gum extracted from the trunk of this tree has effectively been used to treat diarrhea and urinary ailments (Usvat 2014).

Palm oil harvesting is a major cause of deforestation and displacing species like the orangutan, pygmy elephant, and Sumatran rhino.

Caution: Betel nuts have shown evidence of serious health effects from regular use. The sago palm is a cute dwarf palm, but it is poisonous to children and pets.

Practical Uses: Dates and coconuts are used as food and natural medicine. The palm tree leaves are used for shelters and making fires. Tables, chairs, beds, and other furniture can also be made from palm trees. Palm tree wood is pressed to extract oils for soft drinks, cooking, preservatives, syrups, and soaps. The wood fibers are used in hats, parquet flooring, and hammocks. The wood itself is used to construct wicker furniture (Russel 2021). *Kallu*, also known as palm wine, is a common alcoholic spirit in Asia and Africa.

Conservation: Palm oil supplies 35 percent of the world's vegetable oil demand on 10 percent of the land. It is an extremely efficient product. However, palm oil harvesting is a major cause of deforestation and the displacement of species like the orangutan, pygmy elephant, and Sumatran rhino. There is also the concern for releasing greenhouse gases into the atmosphere, contributing to climate change. And there is grave concern about the exploitation of workers and child labor. The Roundtable of Sustainable Palm Oil or RSPO was formed in 2004 in response to increasing concerns about the impacts of palm oil on the environment and society. Things can change if these guidelines are strictly followed (WWF 2020).

Pine (*Pinus*)

Pine (*Pinus*)

There are 126 species of pine tree—some of them live to be a thousand years old and reach a height of 250 feet. Most pines, however, are happy under 150 feet. Pines can exist on little water in full sun. It can also grow 13,000 feet above sea level and color mountain tops green with its branches. As we mentioned in a previous chapter, the oldest known pine is a Bristlecone Pine, dating back five thousand years. It lives in the Inyo National Forest of California.

Pine branches grow laterally and flat from the center trunk. These star-shaped growths are called *whorls*, and the tree can grow one or two of those each year. Pine needles serve as the leaves and stay on the tree full-time, hence the name *evergreen*.

In Korea, the pine tree is seen as a divine, wise being. It makes the coffins of the dead to transport them into the afterlife safely.

In China, the pine tree is regarded as *song shù* (松树), or just *sōng*. It represents longevity, virtue, and solitude. The pine tree is also a popular symbol of the new year.

The pine was the sacred tree of the Mithraic cult of ancient Rome. During the Roman holiday of Saturnalia (December 17–25), the Romans decorated pine trees with ornaments such as *oscilla* made in the image of Bacchus and little clay dolls known as *sigillaria*.

Vast amounts of Scots pines grow across the Scottish countryside. In ancient Druid rituals, the pine was burned to commemorate the changing seasons and to send a signal for the sun to return. Scots pine lumber is especially durable and water-repellent. Shipbuilding in Scotland and the UK thrived for many centuries making pinewood, sea-worthy vessels. Many castles in Scotland and the UK featured tall pines around them (Trufaith7 Apr).

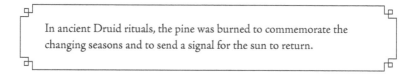

In ancient Druid rituals, the pine was burned to commemorate the changing seasons and to send a signal for the sun to return.

Symbolism: Immortality, eternity, fertility, enlightenment, resurrection, and regeneration

Essential Oil: Pine needle oil is readily available. It is steam-distilled from pine needles and has a brilliant aroma straight from the forest. It helps with respiration and congestion. It has antiseptic, astringent, antibacterial, and anti-inflammatory properties.

Gemstone: Green variscite—intellect, grounding, wealth

Magic: Pine nuts are used in enchantments to attract economic prosperity. Mix needles with resin and burn to ward off spirits. Create a magical healing circle by placing evenly spaced pinecones in a circle around your sacred space or altar.

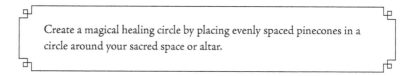

Create a magical healing circle by placing evenly spaced pinecones in a circle around your sacred space or altar.

Notable Associations: Rhea, Cybele, Dionysus, Thor, Attis

Medicine: Pine resin can be used as an antiseptic, astringent, antibacterial, and anti-inflammatory agent. It can be used like Super Glue in the woods to seal cuts and stop bleeding if it is the only first aid available. Needle tea is good for health, having antioxidants, vitamins A and C, and flavonoids.

Caution: Pine tree needles from more than twenty species are poisonous to cattle, humans, and domestic animals. Pregnant women, or those wishing to become pregnant, should avoid pine products and tea.

Practical Uses: Christmas trees! Also, flooring, furniture, coffins, paneling, roofing, shipbuilding, and construction. Some species have large seeds called pine nuts that are highly nutritious and high in amino acids and proteins. Pine tree scent is used in cleaning products and room deodorizers. Pine essential oil is favored for having properties that are anti-inflammatory, antimicrobial, pain-relieving, and congestion relieving. Do not diffuse around cats and dogs, as they could experience harm from the oil molecules in the air (Caro 2021).

Conservation: Pine trees are harvested after thirty years of growth. However, the Chilean pine, the Torrey pine, white bark pine, and Fraser fir are endangered.

Redwood (*Sequoia sempervirens*)

Redwood (*Sequoia sempervirens*)

All hail the ancient ones! Redwoods have been around for about 240 million years. Humans have only been around for about 200,000 years. Big difference. These trees are also the tallest tree on Earth, growing just under four hundred feet.

Redwoods grow in only one place on Earth: A strip along California's Pacific coast. Their girth is massive, their height is breathtaking, but their root system is only six to twelve feet deep. These brilliant redwoods form an underground network intertwined with the roots of other trees, like holding hands, to create strength and endurance. They also speak to one another via this network, share nutrients, and work together to survive.

The bark can be one to two feet thick. The redwoods have special tannins that prevent rot and insect destruction. The *metasequoia*, also known as the Dawn Redwood, was thought to be extinct. In 1941, it was found living in China and is considered to be a living fossil from 150 million years ago.

It is said that to walk among the redwoods is to walk inside nature's cathedral. In many places, the trees form majestic circles resembling earthly cathedrals.

Symbolism: Longevity, strength, vitality, resurrection, eternity, heaven and Earth (connection)

Essential Oil: Redwood needle essential oil is available. However, the quality and purity of private distillation and extraction cannot be guaranteed.

Gemstone: Unakite—vision, balance, grounding

Magic: Draw the heavenly magic into the earth and vice versa. Use a redwood wand as a sacred tool from nature's cathedral. Redwood chips can be burned as a special tribute in spells for longevity and strength.

Notable Associations: Thor, Orion, Hercules

Medicine: The gummy sap is used as a stimulant and tonic to treat fatigue, stress, and depleted conditions. Needle tea can be used as an expectorant.

Caution: Pregnant women and breastfeeding women should not use redwood products.

Practical Uses: Brownish dye can be made from the bark. Sprouts from burls are good for making baskets. The wood is disease- and rot-resistant.

Conservation: Approximately 95 percent of the California redwood forest, which formerly reached across the Santa Cruz Mountains, was logged to build (and rebuild) cities like San Francisco and San Jose.

In 1819, Walt Whitman wrote "The Song of The Redwood Tree" in which he decried the destruction of this fine specimen by loggers.

The wildfire at the Big Basin Redwoods State Park in August 2020 damaged many redwood trees in the hot blaze. However, they will recover, and the forest is now resetting itself for the future. The redwood tree is on the endangered species list because of fire and human destruction.

Studies have shown that coastal redwoods capture more carbon dioxide (CO_2) from our cars, trucks, and power plants than any other tree on Earth. By protecting our local redwood forests, we make a major contribution toward stabilizing our global climate.

How to Ground Yourself Like a Tree

This is a good practice when you feel scattered, insecure, grieving, anxious, or needing to cleanse yourself and your energy field. This process will ground you, remove any negative or heavy feelings, and infuse you with light and spiritual connection.

Directions

1. Remove your shoes and place your bare feet on the ground.
2. Close your eyes and envision yourself as an electromagnetic field.
3. Picture your favorite tree in your mind's eye.
4. Visualize Earth's energy rising into the root system of the tree. Now feel the same energy coming into your feet, emanating from the core of the earth. Allow the energy to rise through your legs and into your body, neck, shoulders, and head.
5. Feel the energy cleansing you as it moves through your body, pulsing and refreshing everything inside. The earth has a steady supply of energy to give and release to you.
6. Release all tension, negative thoughts and feelings, judgments, and grudges. Become one with the energy.

7. When you have connected with the energy, gently change it to golden light.

8. Allow the golden light to take on sparkles and let it flood your mind, body, and soul.

9. Accept this energy into the deepest recesses of your heart and soul. You are like a tree taking in the earth energy and storing it inside.

10. Lock that golden light and energy inside you. Create an inner storehouse to access whenever you need it.

11. When you are ready, open your eyes and know that you are strong and healthy, as your favorite tree, with enough energy and light to supply to others.

Rowan *(Sorbus aucuparia)*

Rowan *(Sorbus aucuparia)*

Related to the rose family (*Rosaceae*), the rowan is a fruit-bearing tree with bright orange or red fruit in most species and bears pink, yellow, or white in some Asian species. The fruit is soft and juicy.

Rowan was one of nine sacred trees burned by the Celts during Beltane and Imbolc celebrations to symbolize new beginnings. Rowan branches are displayed in homes for protection and planted in cemeteries to shield the dead from evil spirits. Rowan trees that grew out of older trees or on unlikely rock crevices were called Flying Rowans (epiphyte) and considered especially powerful because they were seen as airborne and had never touched the ground. These rowans carried extra magical power. The rowan, hawthorn, and elder trees are designated fairy trees. Tradition forbids the cutting of the rowan tree for any purposes other than sacred.

Rowans have a striking appearance, an otherworldly look, and have long been associated with fairies, protection, the feminine, intuition, and psychic abilities (Nykos 2021).

In Nordic lore, the first woman is said to have been born of the rowan tree.

> *Flying Rowans* carried extra magical power. The rowan, hawthorn, and elder trees are designated fairy trees.

Ogham: Second consonant—Luis

Symbolism: Psychic power, death, rebirth, protection against enchantment, fairy magic

Essential Oil: Rowan berries and bark are decocted, but no known essential oil exists other than some for magical purposes.

Gemstone: Dragon's Bloodstone—strength, courage, confidence, endurance, and focus

Magic: The rowan tree will help you see visions beyond this world.

Planting a rowan tree in your front garden wards off witches. A healthy crop of rowan berries on the trees signifies a cold, harsh winter ahead. A rowan wand carries super magical powers. The staffs of the Druids were made from rowan. Finding a rowan wand is a key to powerful magical work.

> Finding a rowan wand is key to powerful magical work because it carries supernatural powers.

Notable Associations: Thor, Hebe, witches, Ravdna, Brighid, fairies

Medicine: Fresh rowan berry juice is usable as a laxative, as a gargle for sore throats, inflamed tonsils, hoarseness, and as a source of vitamins A and C. Rowan berry jam has been known to remedy diarrhea (Kiddle 2021).

Caution: If eaten raw, rowan fruit can affect the liver and kidneys negatively.

Practical Uses: Rowan berries can be a substitute for coffee beans, are used in alcoholic beverages, as a flavoring for liqueurs and cordials, in the production of country wine, and to flavor ale. In the UK, most of the fruit is gathered from wild trees growing on public lands.

Conservation: According to a study, more than half of Europe's endemic trees are threatened with extinction as invasive diseases, pests, pollution, and urban development take a growing toll on the landscape.

Ash, elm, and rowan trees are among those in decline, says an assessment of the continent's biodiversity, which could complicate efforts to tackle the climate crisis through reforestation (Watts 2019).

Sassafras *(Sassafras Albidum)*

Sassafras *(Sassafras Albidum)*

The sassafras tree is a captivating tree known for its brilliant autumn foliage and aromatic smell. Sassafras can be grown as a single-trunk tree or as a dense, bushy thicket. It fruits in the fall, giving dark, blue, berry-like fruit.

Usually, they grow to twenty to sixty feet high and twenty-five to forty feet wide. Its leaves are small, only five to seven inches, and are polymorphic, meaning three-lobed, mitten-shaped, or egg-shaped, with usually only three lobes on each leaf.

In the New World, Native Americans used sassafras extensively for food and medicine long before European settlers arrived. Sassafras bark was one of the first exports of the New World. In the South, the roots were boiled, then combined with molasses, and allowed to ferment into the first root beer. Today sassafras is grown throughout the world. Sassafras has an exotic smell and flavor and is a good repellent of mosquitos.

The leaves and barks of the tree can be used to obtain essential oil through steam distillation.

Symbolism: For the tri-lobed leaf: prosperity, healing, tenacity, whimsy, changes, fairies, and the triple goddess.
The single leaf: the maiden. The mitten shape: the mother.
The triple leaf: the crone, Imbolc, Beltane, and Samhain, respectively.

Artemis is the waxing moon or maiden, Selene the full moon or mother, and Hecate the waning moon or crone. These distinctions mirror the trinity or threefold nature of the triple goddess throughout other pantheons (Sosa 2020).

> Artemis is the waxing moon or maiden, Selene the full moon or mother, and Hecate the waning moon or crone; the trinity or threefold nature of the triple goddess throughout most pantheons, as illustrated by the shapes of the sassafras leaves.

Essential Oil: Sassafras oil is available in essential oil and fragrance oil. However, the quality and purity of private distillation and extraction cannot be guaranteed. Comparable essential oil is Palo Sant (*Bursera graveolens*).

Gemstone: Baltic amber—spontaneity, wisdom, balance, self-expression, patience

Magic: Burn sassafras leaves with oak products for sexual magic. Use leaves for channeling energy. Call in the sassafras muse for inspiration and creative help. Use sassafras to lighten a mood.

Notable Associations: Tridevi (Saraswati, Lakshmi, Kali), Charities (Graces), Horae, Moirai (Fates) Norns, representations of the three aspects of One being

Medicine: Native Americans and early settlers considered sassafras to be a cure-all for all sorts of ailments, from headaches to malaria, fever, liver problems, stomach aches, and colds. Native American women used sassafras to ease menstrual cramps and the after pains of childbirth. They also rubbed the juice on sore joints.

Caution: The roots and bark of the sassafras tree have a toxin called safrole, which can be harmful if taken in large amounts.

Practical Uses: Sassafras wood has been used for furniture because the wood weathers well and is durable. The root oil is used for fragrance, soups, and stews for an unusual extra flavor and exotic taste. The tree has been used to make teas—*saloop*, pink in color—and tonics. The roots have been used to make root beer. The bark makes an orange dye for cloth.

Conservation: Sassafras is listed in the IUCN's Red List of vulnerable and endangered species. A great deal is due to the illegal use of products from the tree, like safrole, which is used to make ecstasy, Molly, and MDMA. It is estimated that 95 percent of the world's sassafras oil is produced from trees that cause deforestation because they are harvested for their oil. It is a hazardous harvesting technique resulting in massive tree destruction. Sassafras oil is now banned but still sold on the black market. The saving grace for the sassafras tree may be in the synthetic production of safrole, which has yet to be created. The best advice is to look at, but don't touch, the sassafras tree.

Willow *(Salix)*

Willow *(Salix)*

The elegant willow tree can grow ten feet per year. It adores water and pops up in flooded areas. It has a deep, wide root system and is a godsend for preventing erosion. There are more than four hundred species of the *Salix* tree.

Weeping willow got its name because when rain falls off the branches, it looks like falling tears. The willow is relatively short-lived and has a life span of about thirty years.

Children love to climb the willow tree because of its friendly and welcoming curved arms. Deer often rub new antlers against the bark of willow trees to relieve the itch because the bark contains salicylic acid—aspirin—and it works as a pain reliever for sprouting horns.

Willows have a serious bent, as well. They have appeared as symbols of death and loss and can also bring magic and mystery to mind. William Shakespeare wrote the "Willow Song" in *Othello*. Desdemona sings the song in her despair. In *Hamlet*, poor Ophelia makes the mistake of sitting on a willow branch by the river and falls in and drowns when it breaks off.

In Greek mythology, the willow goes hand-in-hand with magic, sorcery, and creativity. Hecate, one of the most powerful figures in the underworld, taught witchcraft, and she was the goddess of both the willow and the moon (Grindstaff 2021).

> In Greek mythology, the willow goes hand-in-hand with magic, sorcery, and creativity.

Ogham: Fifth consonant—Saille

Symbolism: Enchantment, immortality, creativity, protection, flexibility, lunar rhythms, healing

Essential Oil: White willow bark oil is available. However, the quality and purity of private distillation and extraction cannot be guaranteed. A comparable essential oil is ho wood (*Cinnamomum camphora*).

Gemstone: Turquoise—Shaman's stone for protection, balance, intuition, friendship

Magic: Use willow branches, leaves, or bark in your new moon practices to increase psychic abilities. Willow is connected to female fertility and can be used in spell work to increase creativity, assist through the passages of life, create and attract love, and bring deep healing from emotional pain. Honor the moon to increase the quantity of love in your life. Braid three willow branches together on the new moon and form a circle. Secure the ends with a red or pink ribbon and place by your bed to attract true love. Willows bend to your desires.

> To attract a new love, braid three willow branches together on the new moon and form a circle. Secure the ends with a red or pink ribbon and place by your bed to attract true love.

Notable Associations: Moon, Selene, Luna, Artemis, Diana, Brighid, Persephone, Hecate

Medicine: The bark of the willow tree produces salicylic acid, the compound found in aspirin. The sap from the tree can be used to avert acne. When steeped in water, the willow tree bark can be used as an infusion or beverage for chills, rheumatism, and bring down fevers.

Caution: People taking anticoagulants should not use willow products. Anyone allergic to aspirin should also not take willow.

Practical Uses: Willow wood and flexible branches are perfect for making baskets, fishing nets, furniture, toys, cricket bats, crates, flutes, whistles, and dye. Native Americans used willow saplings to make their sweat lodges and wigwams.

Conservation: In some parts of the Eastern US, the willow is endangered.

Yew *(Taxus)* *(Taxus baccata)*

Yew *(Taxus)*

The yew tree can live to be three thousand years old, but you'd never know it. The trunk of the yew tree hollows out naturally as time passes, leaving no tree rings behind to determine its age. This means it wants no trace of how or where it lived. Yet, it is a master of deception because out of the tree hollow sprouts a new tree to grow in its place.

When the Romans first met the yew tree when they invaded England and Ireland, they claimed the yew came straight from out of hell.

The yew is full of magical opposites in that the tree is poisonous to humans, yet it represents protection and longevity. The fact that it could kill and protect humans kept the yew in a special place of strength and power over the Celts. It was one of their most sacred trees for that reason.

One tree in Scotland, the Fortingall Yew in Perthshire, is reputed to be nine thousand years old.

Dwelling within the yew is the yew fairy. She is believed to carry the breath of the ancients with her and opens the doorway to future generations. She can also put you in touch with persons that have passed through the veil and onto the next world. Her gift is perspective, so we see our troubles are slight compared to those of the past. Never cut a yew without her explicit permission, or you may meet your ancestors sooner than you wish.

> The fact that the yew tree could kill and protect humans kept it elevated in a sacred place of strength and power over the Celts.

Ogham: The letter I—Idho

Symbolism: Yggdrasil stood for the meaning of life, nine worlds, rebirth, resilience, otherworldly oracle, purification of the dead, transportation to the afterlife, and guardian of the underworld.

Essential Oil: Yew oil is available. However, the quality and purity of private distillation and extraction cannot be guaranteed. Yew soap is a specialty and quite luxurious. A comparable essential oil is vetiver (*Chrysopogon zizanioides*).

Gemstone: Clear quartz—universal healer, spiritual growth, focus

Magic: The yew tree can do nearly everything. It can bring in helpers from the otherworld, spirits from this world, advisors from the past, ancient wisdom, and courage to face it all. It is excellent for protection spells, warding off enemies, eliciting bravery, and calling in guides. The yew is excellent in helping people transition to the next world. It is resilient and, like the Phoenix, can rise from the ashes. A yew wand is a prized and precious thing indeed.

Notable Associations: Artemis, Persephone, Hecate, Astarte, Odin; the yew embodies the crone aspect of the triple goddess

Medicine: Taxol is a miracle cure from the yew tree. It is used in cancer treatment. The red berries are the only thing from the tree that isn't poisonous.

Despite deadly warnings about the yew, it has been used in the past for treating diphtheria, tonsillitis, epilepsy, rheumatism, urinary and liver conditions, and causing abortions.

Caution: The magical irony about this tree is that every part of it is poisonous to humans, domestic animals, and birds. A mere ounce of the needles can be lethal to humans and result in an intoxication, causing heart failure, respiratory paralysis, and liver damage. Horses have been known to die within minutes of eating a few branches. The only nontoxic part of the tree is the red berries from the feminine yew tree. The male tree does not bear fruit. Yet, Taxol has been discovered in the tree and is now used to treat breast, ovarian, and lung cancers.

Practical Uses: Shields and weaponry made from the yew were highly prized by the Celts and were thought to be lucky on the battlefield. A yew spearhead was discovered in Essex, United Kingdom, dating to 450,000 BCE. The yew wood served as the chosen material for longbows used in ancient times. The Celts believed that yew wood would bring victory and long life to the warrior. Staves, rods, and other tools used for divination or spiritual rites were made of yew because it was believed this wood would bring in even more potent energetic connections to the ceremony being performed. It was thought the souls from the underworld would whisper through the yew staves during sacred rituals.

Conservation: The North American Pacific yew (*Taxus brevifolia*) is currently rated "near threatened" on the International Union for Conservation of Nature's Red List. Its high Taxol content has led to over-harvesting for use in cancer treatments (Eden Project—Yew 2021).

Yew Tree Magic—Drawing down Woden for Wisdom, Protection and Prosperity

Woden (or Odin) is the god who breathed his breath into the first human beings, giving them life. Our continued breath is his ongoing gift. Our last breath will be given back to him. He is the source of our life and death. Odin hung upside down on the yew tree, Yggdrasil, to receive the Runes.

You will need:

+ Dried needles from the yew tree

+ 1 teaspoon of fresh tobacco

+ A burning bowl

+ A shot of whiskey in a small glass or shot glass

+ Lighting tool (matches, lighter)

+ Candle

+ Wand

Directions:

1. Center yourself.

2. Focus on Woden.

3. Draw a circle around you and your altar. Define it with your wand. Light the candle to begin the ceremony.

4. Holding the wand aloft, say: "*Hail to Woden, giver of life, center of wisdom, all hail. He who hung upon the tree, between the worlds, to receive the truth and bring the Runes. All hail. Hail to the fearless, mighty God and wondrous Lord. All hail to the giver of life. We present these gifts in praise and honor thee.*"

5. Add the yew needles to the burning bowl, followed by the tobacco. Say: "*Accept these humble offerings as a symbol of our devotion, Oh mighty Woden. Hail to the father of us all.* (Light them and burn them.) *Accept these spirits* (place the whiskey on the altar) *for your might, courage, and bravery. Lo that we should be honored by your might. All hail the mighty Woden,*"

6. Focus on your breath. Connect with the giver of life. After a minute, say, "*Bestow your blessings on us tonight. Grant us wisdom that we might know, prosperity that we may thrive, and protection that we may have a long life. All hail to the mighty one. We are supplicants at your feet.*"

7. With your wand, show gratitude, point upward, and say, *"Let it be done by your grace and will. Thank you for your wisdom. All hail you now and the giver of life. We are thus blessed and do receive with thanks."* Make a ritual gesture of completion and closure.

8. Blow out your candle, and return your offerings to the earth.

9. You have now been blessed by Woden.

On the next few pages is a quick reference guide listing the tree name and its spiritual aspects.

Tree Name	Spiritual Aspect
Acacia	Divine authority, spiritual leadership, immortality, psychic connection, protection
Alder	Balanced male-female energy, resurrection, rebirth, self-regulation, healing
Almond	Beauty, fertility, goodness, energy, grief, hidden treasures, hope, clairvoyance
Apple	Winning, conquest, ultimate prize, golden apple, happiness
Ash	Strength, power, divine connection, authority, protection
Aspen	Communication with the next world, protection from spiritual harm, eloquence, peace, anti-theft
Avocado	Rebirth, lust, beauty, ultimate love
Banyan	Immortality, longevity, death, hermit
Baobab	Ancient awareness, divine communication, blessings, earth wisdom, knowledge, spiritual power, sustenance
Beech	Protection of the heart, trust, new growth, unlocking wisdom, nurturing, letting go of old ways, knowledge
Birch	Renewal, protection, new beginnings
Boswellia	Protection, healing, consecration, purification
Cedar	Strength, longevity, eternity, gateway to higher realms, prosperity

Cherry	New awakenings, rebirth, love, romance, going forward
Chestnut	Life, fertility, birth sustenance
Coconut	Tree of Life, food, shelter, liquid nourishment, purity, healing
Coffee	Emotions, changes, transformation, friendship, balance
Cottonwood	Hope, healing, transformation, ancient wisdom, ancestors
Cypress	Immortality, protection, longevity, past lives
Dogwood	Secrets, loyalty, protection, wishes
Elder	Transformation, death, regeneration, healing, protection
Elm	Nobility, open-mindedness, communication, relationships, feminine power
Eucalyptus	Division between heaven and Earth, purification, cleansing, healing
Fig	Fertility, protection, sacredness, enlightenment, strength
Fir	Protection, spiritual honesty, truth, youth, vitality, immortality
Ginkgo	Magic, longevity, fertility, prosperity
Hawthorn	Renewal, fertility, cleansing, married love, balance of opposites, looking deeper, communication with the spirit world
Hazel	Wisdom, chastity, spirituality, prophecy, healing, fertility
Hemlock	Vulnerability, yin, introspection, shelter, inner knowing, radical transformation
Holly	Unconditional love, sacred, reincarnation, protection against evil, material fortune
Jacaranda	Wisdom, wealth, good luck, rebirth
Juniper	Purification of home, funerary rites, banish evil spells, undo curses, protection
Lemon	Fertility, uplifting, happiness, joy, cleansing, love, light, divination
Linden	Tranquility, love, longevity, prophecy

Mahogany	Safety, strength, protection, magic
Magnolia	Adaptability, healing, love, loyalty, rest
Maple	Development, perseverance, vitality, humility, harmony
Mulberry	Balance, defense, bravery, wisdom
Myrtle	Love, longevity, strength, stability, enterprising
Neem	Purification, universal healing
Oak	Strength, authority, cosmic knowledge, balancing, fertility, money, healing
Olive	Peace, wisdom, fertility, prosperity, health, victory, stability, fidelity
Orange	Generosity, wisdom, honor, chastity, purity
Palm	Victory, triumphant, peace, eternal life, resurrection, male strength
Pine	Immortality, eternity, fertility, enlightenment, regeneration
Redwood	Longevity, strength, invincible, vital heaven and Earth connection, eternity
Rowan	Psychic powers, fairy tree, death, rebirth, protection against enchantment
Sassafras	Prosperity, healing, tenacity, whimsy, changes, fairness, triple goddess
Willow	Enchantment, immortality creativity, protection, flexibility, lunar attunement, moon cycles, healing
Yew	Yggdrasil, meaning of life, nine world, rebirth, resilience, other world travel, purification, death, transportation to the afterlife, guardian of the underworld

Chapter Ten

From Tree to Table

Recipes from Trees (with Love!)

Many recipes on the internet include tree products. I am not nearly the pioneer person that many are, but I do work with tree fruits, spices, and saps in my cooking life. I wanted to share with you a few of my favorites.

It is fun experimenting with new and natural products, and I was amazed at the number of people already cooking with tree products and using those natural resources for health and healing.

I am an avid user of natural products and use organic, natural products wherever possible because I wrote two books on essential oils, a cookbook for heart-healthy eating, and two books on Bach Flower remedies for people and animals.

I am including nineteen recipes from tree crops for your enjoyment and experimentation. If you're already a tree product aficionado, some of these may already be on your radar. If this is new to you, please have fun with them! I have left the recipes intact with the original ingredients I learned to cook with. But I do modify many of them and substitute certain ingredients with others to promote a healthier, fat-free diet for myself. You are welcome to experiment and find your comfort level with these recipes.

The recipes include (alphabetically):

- Acacia Blossom Fritters
- Almond Roca
- Apple Pie Bars
- Avocado—Guacamole with a Sriracha Kick
- Baobab Banana Bread
- Cheery Cherry Cobbler
- Chestnuts, Oven Roasted
- Coconut-Lime Almond Bark
- Coffee-Infused Brownies
- Elderberry Syrup
- Hemlock Tree Sap Wound Salve
- Lemon Cleaners
- Linden Tea
- Mouthwatering Olive Crostini
- Mulberry Pie
- Orange Incense for Your Home
- Palm Heart and Artichoke Fried Cakes
- Pine Needle Tea
- Rowan Berry and Apple Jelly

I love how the magic of the forest comes into our homes, and there is no better way to properly invite them into your life than to prepare meals and products with them. There's a little something for everybody in these recipes and, above all, I encourage you to have fun and enjoy the exciting journey from tree to table.

Acacia Blossom Fritters

Ingredients

- 15–20 acacia flower bunches
- 1 cup (150 g) of all-purpose flour (or almond flour)
- 1½ cup of ice-cold sparkling water (yes, it must be sparkling)
- a pinch of salt
- peanut oil for frying
- sea salt for sprinkling
- acacia honey for drizzling + sugar for sprinkling (sweet version)

Directions

1. Pick fresh acacia blossoms and clean them from dirt or insects.

2. Mix flour and salt in a bowl.

3. Slowly, using a small stream, pour sparkling water into the mixture.

4. Stir with a whisk, removing all lumps.

5. Add 1 to 2 inches of peanut oil to a pan wide enough to accommodate the blossoms. Heat the oil to 350°F (175°C).

6. Holding the flowers by their stems, dip them into the batter.

7. Carefully shake off excess batter. You want them light and fluffy.

8. Gently place your flowers in the oil and allow them to fry to a golden brown. Don't crowd the pan. Once they have cooked on one side, flip them over, using a slotted spoon. Watch for a golden-brown color to know they are done.

9. Remove the fried flowers from the oil and place them on paper towels to absorb the excess oil. Lightly sprinkle with salt or drizzle with honey or dust with sugar or stevia for a sweeter treat.

Almond Roca

Allow me to set the scene and explain why this is a special recipe. My father guarded it all his life, but now I can share it with you. Imagine a snowy, blustery day in early December in the Pacific Northwest. You could count on rain and snow this time of year when I grew up in Bellingham, Washington. Snow was a critical part of my dad's recipe.

Each Christmas my father would make his famous Almond Roca for our neighbors and friends and us. Everyone was my dad's friend, so he made several big batches every year and gave them away as gifts. He was famous for his Almond Roca and generous heart.

It was a family affair—me, my mom, and my dad. I would chop the nuts, dad would cook up the bubbling toffee and stir the pot, and my mother would continually warn us not to burn ourselves. My dad always cooled his candy on the back of the car in the carport, which was covered with snow. It cooled faster that way and we got to eat it sooner. If you don't have snow around when you make yours, the refrigerator will do nicely. I'm not even going to mention the nutritional benefits because it was Christmas, and we were celebrating. You will have to be your own portion monitor.

Almond Roca Secret Family Recipe

You will need a heavy pan, a wooden spoon, and a candy thermometer for this recipe, plus the ingredients.

Ingredients

- 2 cups chopped toasted almonds, divided
- 1 cup packed light brown sugar
- 2 sticks salted butter—no substitutes or it won't work
- 2 cups milk chocolate or semi-sweet chocolate chips (buy the good stuff; it makes a big difference)

Directions

1. Toast the almonds in a pan or oven to get them slightly golden brown. (Be careful not to burn them.)

2. Cool and then and chop the almonds into semi-coarse bits.

3. Coat a high-edged, nine-by-twelve-inch cookie sheet with butter.

4. Sprinkle 1 cup of toasted almonds on bottom of the pan.

5. In a heavy saucepan, melt butter on medium heat, frequently stirring as not to burn. Add brown sugar when butter has melted. Stir until gently boiling. Reduce heat to medium or medium-low. Set your timer to boil for 10 minutes precisely while stirring without ceasing. This is a crucial stage. Your toffee can burn in an instant if you don't keep stirring or if your candy thermometer isn't in the pot.

6. Pull your pot off the heat when it has reached the hard-crack stage (290–300°F), or when the oil starts to separate from the sugar. You'll know. If you let your mixture reach 320°F, you will have soft candy and not the crisp kind that we want. (Don't look away for a second. This is critical candy-making!)

7. Remove your mixture from the heat; boldly stir it one more time to mix up the butter and sugar. Pour the hot mixture over the almonds on the cookie sheet. Use hot pads to make sure you have a firm grip and don't spill this mixture. It *will* burn you.

8. Wait a few minutes for the mixture to set up. When the top part is almost hard to the touch, you can score the setting candy with a long knife so you can break it into even squares. (Skip this step if you don't care about uniformity.)

9. Chill the cooling mixture out in the cold if that's your part of the country or use the refrigerator. When the mixture has completely cooled (30 to 60 minutes), bring it out and set it on the counter. Wipe off the top of the Almond Roca if a buttery film has coated the top. This will help the chocolate topping adhere better.

10. In a double boiler, melt your chocolate chips carefully, and when it is spreadable, pour it onto the toffee in the pan, smooth with a spatula, and quickly sprinkle the rest of the almonds on top.

11. Sprinkle with the remaining toasted almonds and gently press them into the chocolate.

12. Now, for the hard part. You must wait until this mixture has cooled again before breaking the Almond Roca apart into chunks with a sharp knife. Store in a covered container. My dad liked to use tins with foil sheets between the layers.

Please enjoy this recipe and think of my dad, the Irish leprechaun, when you smack your lips and smile.

Apple Pie Bars

Ingredients
For the crust (you can also use a premade crust for this recipe)

- Cooking spray
- 1 cup (2 sticks) butter, softened
- ½ cup granulated sugar
- ¼ cup packed light brown sugar
- 2½ cups all-purpose flour
- ½ teaspoon kosher salt

For the filling

- 6 apples, peeled, cored, and sliced
- Juice of ½ lemon
- ½ cup packed brown sugar
- 1 teaspoon ground cinnamon
- 1 teaspoon pure vanilla extract
- ½ teaspoon kosher salt

For the topping

- 1½ cups all-purpose flour
- 1 cup chopped pecans
- 1 cup packed brown sugar
- ½ teaspoon kosher salt
- ¾ cup (1½ sticks) butter, melted
- Caramel, for serving (premade in the jar)

Directions

1. Preheat the oven to 350°F and line a nine-by-thirteen-inch pan with parchment. Then grease with cooking spray. In a large bowl using a hand mixer, beat butter and sugars together until light and fluffy. Add flour and salt and mix until just combined.

2. Press into the prepared pan about half an inch up the sides. Bake until lightly golden, or 20 minutes.

3. In a large bowl, toss apples, lemon juice, brown sugar, cinnamon, vanilla, and salt together. Spread apple mixture over the crust.

4. In a medium bowl, whisk together flour, pecans, brown sugar, and salt. Stir in melted butter until coarse clumps form.

5. Sprinkle crumb topping over apples and bake until the top is golden and apples are soft, about 1 hour.

6. Let cool at least 15 minutes, then slice into squares and drizzle with caramel before serving.

Avocado Guacamole with a Sriracha Kick

Ingredients

- 4 ripe avocados
- 3 medium tomatoes, ripe
- 1 clove finely minced garlic
- 1 cup chopped sweet onion
- 2 teaspoons fresh lemon juice
- 1 teaspoon white wine vinegar (or regular white vinegar if you prefer)
- 1 tablespoon sriracha sauce
- ½ teaspoon kosher salt (add salt to taste, but remember to use sparingly)
- ¼ teaspoon fresh ground pepper

Directions

1. Remove skin and pits from avocados. Dice avocadoes into small pieces.
2. Finely mince one medium-size clove of fresh garlic.
3. Dice the tomatoes into small pieces.
4. Dice the onion into small pieces.
5. Combine onion, avocados, and tomatoes with salt, pepper, garlic, vinegar, sriracha, and lemon juice. Mix well. Taste. You can also add a little more lemon juice if you prefer a tarter taste.
6. Serve with anything you want: veggies, home-baked tortilla chips, home-baked whole wheat pita triangles, or top a chicken taco salad. Yum.

Baobab Banana Bread

Ingredients

- 3 medium overripe bananas (mashed into large chunks)
- 1 cup dairy or nondairy milk (almond or oat is fine)
- ¼ cup vegetable, sunflower, or light olive oil
- 1 teaspoon apple cider vinegar (can use lemon juice instead)
- 1 teaspoon vanilla extract
- 1½ cups Baobab Powder
- ½ cup light brown sugar
- 1 teaspoon baking powder
- ½ teaspoon baking soda
- ½ teaspoon salt
- 1 teaspoon cinnamon
- Dash of nutmeg

Directions

1. Preheat oven to 350°F.
2. Grease nine-by-five-inch nonstick loaf pan with vegetable oil or cooking spray.
3. Using a large bowl, mash the bananas into chunks; add vanilla, oil, milk, and apple cider vinegar.

4. Mix until well combined.

5. In a medium bowl, combine flour, baobab powder, sugar, baking soda, cinnamon, nutmeg, salt, and baking powder.

6. Combine wet ingredients with dry ingredients and fold until just combined. Do not over mix.

7. Pour into your greased baking pan and bake for 45 to 55 minutes or until a toothpick comes out clean from center of bread.

8. Let loaf cool before removing from pan (10 to 20 minutes).

A Little Bit About Cherries

Trees produce over one hundred types of cherries. Generally, cherries are classified based on their sweetness or tartness—*sweet* or *sour* cherries.

The most popular sweet cherry types are dark red Bing cherries, deep black Chelan cherries, and sweet dark cherries known as Lapins. In the sour category there are Montmorency cherries and Morello cherries. Apart from having red or dark red skins, other types of sweet cherries have yellow skins with a light red blushing and yellow flesh. I have chosen a *sour cherry* recipe for you.

Cheery Cherry Cobbler

Initially, preheat your oven to 350°F.

Ingredients

Wet mixture

- 5 cups sour cherries (like Montmorency cherries)
- 2 tablespoons cornstarch
- ¾ cup sugar, plus 2 tablespoons, divided

Dry mixture—topping

- 1½ cups flour
- ½ teaspoon fine sea salt
- 1½ teaspoons baking soda
- 4 tablespoons unsalted butter
- ½ cup milk

> **Note:** For a shortcut, you can use Bisquick instead of making the biscuits from scratch.

Topping alternative with Bisquick

- 1 cup Bisquick mix
- ¼ cup milk
- ¼ cup sugar
- 2 tablespoons butter melted

Mix together and dollop onto the wet mixture in place of the biscuits. Top with ice cream, whipped cream, or frozen yoghurt for serving.

Directions

1. Combine the cherries, ¾ cup of sugar, and cornstarch in a bowl. Stir softly to combine.

2. Let the fruit macerate for 30 minutes while preparing the biscuit dough. (If you are using the Bisquick mix, follow the cobbler directions on the back of the box instead of below.)

3. In a medium bowl, whisk together the flour, salt, baking soda, and remaining sugar.

4. Slice the butter thinly, toss it in the dry mixture, and cut in with a metal pastry blender.

5. Drizzle the milk slowly to moisten the dough and gently stir to combine. Stir enough to combine but no more. (You want fluffy not tuffy.)

6. Place on a lightly floured board and knead five to six times to merge ingredients.

7. With a pastry roller, roll out dough to be a half-inch thick.

8. Cut into biscuit rounds (use a floured glass or a biscuit cutter).

9. Pour the cherry mixture into a casserole or baking dish and top with the biscuit rounds.

10. Bake until the biscuits are golden and the cherry juices have bubbled and are thickened, about 45 minutes.

11. Allow to cool for 15 to 30 minutes before serving.

12. Top with whipped cream and or ice cream. French vanilla is awesome.

Chestnuts, Oven Roasted

Roasting is one of the best ways to enjoy chestnuts. Bitter when raw, roasted chestnuts have a delicate and slightly sweet flavor with a soft texture like sweet potato. They're especially popular around the Christmas holidays and easy to make at home. (Make sure you are not using horse chestnuts, which are poisonous.) Recipe takes about 20 minutes to prep and finish.

Ingredients

*   ½ pound chestnuts, unpeeled and unroasted

Directions

1. Heat the oven to 425°F.
2. Using a sharp paring knife, make an X-shaped cut on the round side of each chestnut. (This critical step keeps them from exploding from internal pressure when heated and makes peeling easier after roasting.)
3. Arrange chestnuts on a baking rack or a baking sheet.
4. Transfer the chestnuts to the oven and roast them until the skins have pulled back from the cuts and the nutmeats have softened.
5. The actual time required will depend on the chestnuts but will be at least 15 to 20 minutes.
6. Remove the nuts from the oven and pile them into a mound in an old towel.
7. Wrap them up, squeeze hard—the chestnuts should crackle—and let them sit for a few minutes.
8. Pull and snap off the dark shells to reveal the yellowish-white chestnuts. While peeling, make sure to also remove the papery skin between the shell and the chestnut.

Coconut-Lime Almond Bark

Ingredients

- 1 package (10–12 ounces) white chocolate baking chips
- 4 teaspoons coconut oil
- 2 to 4 drops green food coloring
- ½ cup sweetened shredded coconut, lightly toasted
- ½ cup chopped almonds, toasted
- 1–2 tablespoons grated lime zest
- 2 drops natural lime oil for cooking
- You can add ½ cup cranberries and other dried fruits you like

Directions

1. Line a nine-inch-square baking pan with foil; set aside.
2. In a double boiler, melt the chips and coconut oil and stir until smooth.
3. Stir in food coloring, shredded coconut, lime oil, almonds, and lime zest.
4. Spread into the prepared pan.
5. Chill until firm, 10 to 15 minutes.
6. Break into small pieces.
7. Store in an airtight container at room temperature.

Coffee-Infused Brownies

Ingredients

- You will need a packaged brownie mix that calls for water
- Use ingredients described on package
- Measure out the amount of water; only use espresso coffee instead of water
- ½ cup mocha chips
- ¼ cup of walnuts pieces

Directions

1. Mix all ingredients together following package instructions.
2. Add the mocha chips and walnuts to the prepared batter and stir to combine.
3. Pour into eight- or nine-inch baking pan.
4. Bake according to package instructions.
5. Cool and serve.

Elderberry Syrup

Traditionally, elderberry is most often taken as a supplement to treat cold and flu symptoms. (Caution: too much can cause stomach issues.)

Ingredients

- ¾ cup dried elderberries
- 3 cups water
- 1 teaspoon dried cinnamon or 1 cinnamon stick
- 1 teaspoon dried cloves or 4 whole cloves
- 1 tablespoon fresh ginger or 1 teaspoon dried ginger
- 1 cup raw honey

Directions

1. In a large pot, bring the elderberries, water, cinnamon, cloves, and ginger to a boil.

2. Reduce the heat, cover, and simmer until the liquid has reduced by half, about 40 to 45 minutes.

3. Allow the liquid to cool, and then drain the liquid using a fine-mesh strainer or cheesecloth.

4. Press all liquid out of the berries using the back of a wooden spoon. Discard skins.

5. Add the raw honey to the liquid and mix well.

6. Store in an airtight glass container in the refrigerator for up to two months.

Hemlock Tree Sap Wound Salve

For External Use Only

Equipment

*   Double boiler or Pyrex 1- or 2-cup measure
*   Saucepan
*   Strainer or sieve
*   Metal or glass containers
*   Wooden spoon for stirring

Ingredients

*   Dried sap or resin (about the size of a penny or nickel)
*   2 oz. jojoba, apricot kernel, carrot seed, avocado, or olive oil
*   1–2 oz. beeswax chips, flakes, or pellets

Directions

1. Collect some dried sap (resin) from a wounded eastern hemlock tree.

2. Using a double boiler, heat the sap until it becomes liquid. (Never heat the pine sap directly over a flame because it will burst into flames.)

3. Strain the heated pine sap through a sieve to remove dirt, bark, or particles.

4. Once again, in the double boiler, add in 1 to 2 oz. chosen oil, depending on the size of your piece of resin. Combine in the double boiler.

5. Add 1 oz. beeswax chips, flakes, or pellets to add firmness.

6. You may need to add more oil or more beeswax to get the oure you want.

7. I like to test the mixture at this point. I spoon a little into a small jar or tin and wait for it to harden. Once it has solidified, I check it for texture. If it is too soft, I add more beeswax; too hard, I add more oil.

> **Note:** this recipe can be used for any pine or conifer resin you find in nature.

Lemon Cleaners

Lemons have an incredible range of household uses. Here are a few.

Clean copper-bottom pots and pans: You can clean your copper-bottomed pots and pans with lemon juice. Copper fixtures, like lights and colanders, can also benefit from a lemon juice cleaning. Cut a lemon in half. Dip it in some salt and clean spots from your copper. This same mixture of lemon juice and salt can also be used to clean coffee makers, microwaves, and food storage containers.

Add the mixture to vinegar: Although vinegar can be a great cleaning ingredient, it can have a disagreeable scent. Adding lemon juice to vinegar when cleaning will neutralize the vinegar smell.

Countertops: Countertop stains can be removed by squeezing lemon juice and allowing it to sit on the stain for a few minutes. Scrub the area with a little baking soda on a sponge and watch the stains disappear. Tip: Don't leave the lemon juice sitting for too long on your countertop. It can do damage if left unchecked.

Drains: Lemon rinds can be ground in your garbage disposal to freshen the drain. Hot water with a little lemon juice poured into the drain will freshen it.

Bleaching: Lemon juice is a natural bleaching agent. Spray a little lemon juice onto white linens and white clothing and allow them to dry in the sun. Stains will be naturally bleached away.

Degreasing: The acid in lemon juice cuts right through grease and is excellent for removing grease from the stove and countertops.

Glass Cleaning: With or without vinegar, lemon is an effective glass cleaner. If you decide to add vinegar to the solution, the pleasant smell of lemon overrides the vinegar smell.

Linden Tea

known as *Tilleul* in France

Preparations

- Find a linden tree in your yard, neighborhood, or park.
- Strip leaves off a branch along with buds and flowers.
- Trim back stripped branch.
- Make sure the leaves dry either in the shade or on paper towels.
- Steam the leaves (like you would vegetables) on your stove for about a minute. (For a different flavor, try roasting them in a skillet for 2 minutes instead of steaming.)
- Spread the leaves, buds, and flowers on a baking sheet and dry them in the oven at 250°F for 20 minutes. Check after 20 minutes. If they are not crispy, add another 10 minutes.
- Allow the leaves to cool, maybe overnight, and then store them in an airtight container. Make sure they are completely dried and cooled before storing.

Make Your Tea:

1. Place a small handful of the dried leaves in each cup. Add boiling water. Steep to the color you wish, strain, and drink. If making in a teapot, experiment with how much of the dried leaves you need to reach the color you prefer.

2. This tea goes well with baklava, honey lace cookies, or a lovely cinnamon spice cake.

Mouthwatering Olive Crostini

Ingredients

*   1 can (4¼ oz) chopped ripe olives (or brined and aged)
*   1 can (4¼ oz) chopped black olives (or olive of your choice)
*   ⅛ teaspoon chili flakes
*   ½ cup grated parmesan cheese
*   ¼ cup butter, softened
*   1 tablespoon olive oil
*   2 garlic cloves, minced
*   ¾ cup shredded part skim mozzarella cheese
*   ¼ cup minced fresh parsley
*   1 French baguette, sliced in quarter-inch slices

Directions

1. Mix all of the ingredients (except the baguette) together.
2. Preheat oven to 400°F.
3. Place the sliced bread onto a cookie sheet.
4. Brush a light coat of olive oil onto the bread.
5. Cook for 8 to 10 minutes until bead is golden and toasted.
6. Allow to cool for 5 minutes and then spread the mixture onto each bread slice.
7. Reduce oven heat to 350°F.

8. Return cookie sheet and prepared bread slices to the oven and cook for an additional 8 to 10 minutes.

9. Remove from oven, allow to cool for five minutes, transfer to a serving plate, and serve warm.

Mulberry Pie

Ingredients

- 1 prepared pie crust (2 crusts), frozen or packaged
- 3½–4 cups mulberries (fresh or frozen, thawed)
- 1 orange (zested)
- 1 tablespoon orange juice
- 1 tablespoon apple sauce, unsweetened
- 1 cup sugar, raw sugar, date sugar
- ⅓ cup flour or almond flour
- ¼ teaspoon salt
- 1 tablespoon butter or butter substitute

Directions

1. Preheat oven to 375°F.
2. Line the bottom of a nine-inch pie plate with one of the two pie crusts.
3. If using frozen fruit, be sure to let the mixture stand and drain for 45 minutes before mixing.
4. Mix mulberries with orange zest and orange juice.
5. In another bowl, combine sugar, flour, and salt.
6. Stir dry ingredients into the mulberry mixture.
7. Pour the mulberry mixture into the prepared pie crust.
8. Dot with butter, and top with the remaining pie crust. A lattice fashion allows the berries to seep through the crust.

9. Cover the edges of your pie with foil or a pie edge protector. Bake for an hour, or until you can see that the pie is bubbling and begins to ooze out of the crust.

10. Cool before slicing. Enjoy with some vanilla ice cream, frozen yogurt, or whipped cream.

Orange Incense for Your Home

Ingredients

- Dried orange peels (add in lemon or lime if you wish; see recipe below)
- Whole cinnamon sticks
- Whole cloves
- White vinegar
- Sweet orange essential oil (optional)
- Small or medium saucepan

Directions

1. In a small saucepan, add a handful of dried citrus peels, a cinnamon stick, and a few cloves.

2. Cover with a ½-inch to 1 inch of water.

3. Add 2 to 3 tablespoons of vinegar.

4. Bring to a low simmer and leave over a low flame for an hour or two. Check every 20 to 30 minutes in case the water evaporates. The vinegar serves as an air freshener, while the cinnamon, cloves, and oils will fill your space with a warm fragrance. Add a few drops of sweet orange essential oil about halfway through to intensify the scent.

How to Dry Orange Peels

1. Peel several oranges.

2. Place the peels on a parchment-paper-lined cookie sheet.

3. Turn oven on the lowest setting.

4. Place cookie sheet with peels in oven and set for 30 minutes. Check to make sure they are crisp. If not, leave for another 15 minutes. Allow to cool and store in an airtight jar with a lid.

5. With dried orange peels, you can make the incense in the recipe above, and you can also put the dried peels in a blender and blend until you have a finely chopped peel. Use this as seasoning for cooking in meats, desserts, or as a topping.

6. You can also continue to grind the peels into a fine powder suitable and refreshing for using on your face.

Palm Heart and Artichoke-Fried Cakes

Ingredients

For cakes

- 14 oz. canned hearts of palm drained, dried, and chopped
- 14 oz. canned artichoke hearts drained, dried, and chopped
- 2 garlic cloves minced
- 2 teaspoons Italian parsley, minced
- 2 tablespoons dried onions (don't use fresh onions, only dried)
- 1 teaspoon Dijon mustard
- 1 egg, lightly beaten
- ¼ cup mayonnaise
- ¾ cup panko breadcrumbs
- light extra virgin olive oil for frying

Panko crust

- 1 cup panko breadcrumbs (white or wheat)
- 1 teaspoon ground black pepper
- 1 teaspoon fine sea salt

Garnish for serving (optional)

- Garlic aioli
- Lemon wedges
- Fresh bean sprouts
- Hummus

Directions

1. In a large mixing bowl, combine all ingredients for hearts of palm cakes, mixing well.

2. In a shallow dish or pie plate, mix panko crust ingredients: panko breadcrumbs, sea salt, and ground black pepper.

3. Divide cake mix into eight equal mounds. Form each mound into a patty.

4. Place each patty in the panko crust mix, turn, and pat on both sides to cover. Transfer each coated patty to a large plate or baking sheet.

5. Freeze the cakes for 20 to 30 minutes to set them up.

6. Heat olive oil in a frying pan over medium-high heat.

7. Working in two batches, fry cakes in olive oil for 3 to 4 minutes on each side or until lightly browned.

8. Double the layers of paper towels on a serving plate. Add cooked patties to plate to drain.

9. Serve while still hot with garlic aioli, lemon wedges, and hummus.

Pine Needle Tea

Gathering of Needles

Do not pick needles off any pine tree. Yew, Norfolk Island pine, and Ponderous pine are toxic to humans. Make sure you know the tree you are extracting needles from, and make sure you have permission. Suggested pine species are the eastern white pine (*Pinus strobus*) and Douglas fir (*Pseudotsuga menziesii*). It is also best to buy pine needles already harvested for you unless you really know your trees.

Directions

1. Start with clean hands.
2. Wash your needles in clear water. Pat dry.
3. Cut off the ends of your needles and roll them around between your palms to release the oil.
4. Place the needles in a cup.
5. Add 1 cup of boiling water.
6. Steep for 15 minutes.
7. Remove needles and enjoy.
8. Add lemon or honey to taste.

Enjoy your tea and lap up all those healthy vitamins A and C nutrients.

Caution: Pregnant women or women intending on becoming pregnant should not drink this tea.

Rowan Berry and Apply Jelly

Rowan tree fruit typically needs something sweeter to balance their bitter taste. Apples do the trick.

Gather:

- ✦ Rowan fruit: Be on alert because the birds may get them before you do. Pick your berries as soon as they are ripe and freeze ahead.
- ✦ Wash under running cold water.
- ✦ De-stalk the fruit.
- ✦ *Never eat the fruit raw.* This could result in digestive and liver problems.
- ✦ Prepare and sterilize jelly jars for storing the jelly. Set them aside.

Ingredients:

- 3 pounds of rowan berries
- 3 firm apples (cored and chopped Bramley or Granny Smith apples)
- Juice of one lemon
- 6 whole cloves
- 5–6 Juniper berries
- 6 pints cold water
- 3 pounds of sugar

Directions:

1. Place the rowan berries, chopped apples, lemon juice, cloves, and Juniper berries in large soup kettle or stockpot.

2. Cover the fruit with cold water.

3. Boil on high heat, then reduce heat to low and simmer for about half an hour until the berries have almost lost their color and the sugar is dissolved. Turn off the heat, cover, and cool for an hour.

4. Pour the jelly and apple mix into a muslin bag or a jelly bag and hang the bag overnight to drip into a pan below, or you can use a stool to help drain the mixture. Tie twine around the seat of the stool, attach the muslin bag (or jelly bag) full of berries and apples underneath the

stool. Place a drip bowl underneath and leave alone to drip for 12 hours. Or you can use a large sieve and allow the juice to drip through the fruit pulp into bowl below.

5. Next morning, take 4 pints of the rowan apple juice, pour it into a large pot, and add 3 pounds of white sugar to it.

6. Boil on high heat until you reach a simmer. Reduce heat and allow to simmer. You will need to watch your jelly now.

7. As the liquid simmers, a white film may appear. Skim that off. Allow the jelly to simmer for approximately 45 minutes and begin checking for doneness.

8. Test your jelly to see if it is ready to set by taking a spoon full of the liquid out of the pot, allowing it to cool on a plate, and, if it wrinkles, the jelly is ready to go into jars.

9. Carefully ladle the liquid into your jars. Allow to fully cool (to cold) before putting the lids on. Tighten and label.

10. Finished jelly can be stored in a cool, dry place for months. Once opened, the jar needs to be stored in the refrigerator.

11. The flavor of the jelly improves after aging six months.

You now have bragging rights for fresh rowan-apple jelly.

Chapter Eleven

Special Gifts from Trees to Us

Trees have many things to give us besides magic. On the practical level, they give us shelter in the form of lumber, and, in days gone by, branches and leaves for roofing and bedding. Today we utilize their bounty of fruits, berries, seeds, bark, medicines, salves, syrups, corks, latex, sponges, paper, chewing gum, car wax, hair dye, and of course, coffee and chocolate. There are many more gifts that trees give us. Let's explore some of their extra special gifts.

Oxygen

In our grade school science classes we learned about photosynthesis, a process by which plants and trees magically transform carbon dioxide into oxygen. We know that animals and humans exhale carbon dioxide into the atmosphere. Plants and trees crave carbon dioxide and absorb it into their leaves and needles. Inside, it pairs with hydrogen to produce sugar. The tree keeps the sugar as food, and the extra oxygen created during this process is released into the atmosphere. One large tree can supply enough oxygen for one full day for four people (Stancil 2019).

Essential Oils

You may not be aware of the essential oils that come from trees. Let's divide these into sections, specifically, certain parts of the trees that the oils are derived or distilled from. Not all the trees we will mention have been covered in our previous chapters, but some have.

Trees are the bridges between the cosmos and the earth, and their essences help us live in both realms. Some essential oils may be grounding, but some help us rise upward. We'll look at the tree and the human body and discover how many similarities there are. We will begin with the top of the tree and work down to the roots. Each essential oil derived from a part of the tree coincides with a section of the human body and its needs.

Just like the tree, humans breathe from the top of the body. The top of the tree has parts that breathe and convert carbon dioxide into oxygen. We are so much alike, humans and trees.

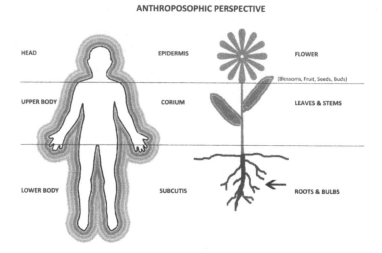

How Trees Help Humans

Leaves and Twigs Essential Oils

These essential oils primarily help with respiratory conditions, nasal congestion, and some act as tick repellants.

Cajeput (white tea tree)	*Melaleuca leucadendra*
Cedar leaf	*Cedrus*
Cinnamon leaf	*Cinnamomum verum*
Eucalyptus: blue gum	*Eucalyptus globule*
Eucalyptus: blue mallee	*Eucalyptus polybractea*

Laurel leaf	*Laurus nobilis*
Tea tree	*Melaleuca alternifolia*
Tea tree (lemon)	*Leptospermum petersonii*
Mandarin	*Citrus reticulata*
Petitgrain	*Citrus aurantium ssp. amara*
Manuka	*Leptospermum scoparium*
Magnolia leaf	*Magnolia grandiflora*
Niaouli	*Melaleuca quinquenervia*
Nerolina	*Melaleuca quinquenervia*
Rosalina	*Melaleuca ericifolia*
Purple sage	*Salvia officinalis*
White sage	*Salvia apiana*
Violet leaf (absolute)	*Viola*
Wintergreen	*Gaultheria procumbens*

Needles and Branches Essential Oils

These essences support the human respiratory system. These are also known for their antibacterial, antiseptic properties and their ability to support the immune system.

Cypress	*Cupressus*
Balsam fir	*Abies lasiocarpa var. lasiocarpa*
Cork bark fir	*Abies lasiocarpa* (Hook.) Nutt
Cork bark Fir, variation	*Abies lasiocarpa var. arizonica* (Merriam) Lemmon
Douglas fir	*Pseudotsuga menziesii*
Hemlock fir	*Abies grandis*
Noble fir	*Abies procera*
Siberian fir needle	*Abies sibirica*

Black pine	*Pinus thunbergii*
Douglas pine	*Pseudotsuga menziesii*
Pinon pine	*Pinus edulis Engelm*
Ponderosa pine	*Pinus ponderosa*
Scotch pine	*Pinus sylvestris*
Norway spruce	*Picea abies*
Red spruce	*Picea rubens*
Sitka spruce	*Picea sitchensis*
Tamarack	*Larix laricina*

Citrus Peel Essential Oils

Citrus peels have been used for centuries in medicinal applications. They possess phytochemical compounds of excellent antimicrobial properties to fight against many bacteria and fungi.

Bergamot	*Citrus bergamia*
Bigarade (Petitgrain)	*Citrus Aurantium*
Grapefruit	*Citrus paradisi*
Lemon	*Citrus × limon*
Lime	*Citrus × aurantiifolia*
Sweet orange	*Citrus X sinensis*
Tangerine	*Citrus reticulata*

Petals Essential Oils

Carnation	*Dianthus caryophyllus*
Champaca	*Magnolia champaca*
Coffee flower	*Coffea*
Jasmine sambac	*Jasminum sambac*

Lotus	*Nelumbo nucifera*
Magnolia	*Magnolia grandiflora*
Narcissus	*Narcisseae*
Neroli	*Citrus aurantium*
Osmanthus	*Osmanthus fragrans*
Rose	*Rosa damascena*
Tuberose	*Polianthes tuberosa*
Ylang-ylang	*Cananga odorata*

Resin Essential Oils

These help the body because they are often anti-viral, antiseptic, and anti-tumoral and are ancient healers.

Balsam copaiba (copal)	*Copaifera officinalis*
Benzoin	*Styrax benzoin*
Elemi	*Canarium luzonicum*
Frankincense	*Boswellia*
Galbanum	*Ferula galbaniflua*
Myrrh	*Commiphora myrrha*
Palo santo	*Bursera graveolens*

Seeds and Berries Essential Oils

These essences often help skin, scars and wrinkles and some address digestion issues. Many are associated with the reproductive organs and cycles.

Argan oil (Moroccan oil)	*Argania spinosa L.*
Cardamon seed	*Elettaria cardamomum Maton*
Coffee (absolute)	*Coffea*
Elderberry	*Sambucus*

Grape seed oil	*Vitis Vinifera*
Juniper berry	*Juniperus communis*
Rose hip seed	*Rosa canina L.*
May chang	*Litsea Cubeba*
Nutmeg	*Myristica fragrans*
Tamanu	*Calophyllum inophyllum*
White cinnamon	*Canella winterana*
Vanilla	*Vanilla planifolia*

Tree Trunks—Wood, Bark, and Heartwood Essential Oils

Many of these essential oils are wound-healing and alleviate the discomforts of muscle aches, joint pain, and stiffness.

Amyris	*Amyris elemifera*
Cade (prickly juniper)	*Juniperus oxycedrus*
Buddha wood	*Eremophila Mitchellii*
Balsam gurjun	*Dipterocarpus turbinatus*
Peru balsam	*Myroxylon balsamum pereirae*
Atlas cedarwood	*Cedrus atlantica*
Himalayan cedarwood	*Cedrus deodara*
Texas cedarwood	*Juniperus mexicana*
Virginia cedarwood	*Juniperus virginiana L.*
Cinnamon bark	*Cinnamomum burmannii*
Blue cypress	*Callitris intratropica*
Guaiacwood	*Guaiacum officinale*
Ocean (maritime) pine	*Pinus pinaster*
Ravensara	*Ravensara aromatica*

Ravintsara	*Cinnamonum camphora*
Indian sandalwood	*Santalum album*
Australian sandalwood	*Santalum spicatum*
Hawaiian sandalwood	*Santalum haleakalae*
Fijian sandalwood	*Santalum yasi*
Zanthoxylum	*Zanthoxylum piperitum*

Roots and Rhizomes Essential Oils

Essential oils from tree roots and rhizomes are inherently centering, calming, and sedating. They can offer pain relief; many are anti-parasitic.

Angelica root	*Angelica archangelica*
Arnica (mountain tobacco)	*Arnica montana*
Curcuma	*Curcuma longa*
Ginger	*Zingiber officinale*
Ginger lily	*Hedychium coronarium*
Calamus	*Acorus calamus*
Spikenard	*Nardostachys jatamansi*
Vetiver	*Chrysopogon zizanioides*
Valerian root	*Valeriana officinalis*

Wishing Trees

Trees have been the instruments of hope and healing in many cultures since the beginning of time. Trees and tree groves were sacred places with magical and healing qualities. Benevolent spirits dwelled within the trees, so why would you not ask a tree when you needed a favor?

Many glorious wishing trees are tucked away in special places around the world. You may be driving in the countryside of Ireland and see a tree festooned with multi-colored scarves, flags, and notes tied to its branches.

In Turkey, wishing trees are commonplace in villages and are thick with hanging requests for money, healing, cures, marriage, and every sort of supplication imaginable.

In Cappadocia, trees are weighted down with glass charms of the famous evil eye talisman to ward off bad luck.

In Essex, United Kingdom, a tree stump is laden with thousands of coins pressed into its bark. Legend says that if you press a coin into the tree, you will be healed. If someone dares to remove a coin from the tree, they will become ill.

You might recall the song "Tie a Yellow Ribbon Round the Old Oak Tree" from 1973. It was a message to a young man, just released from prison, about whether he should get off the bus or keep going. Today, yellow ribbons refer to supporting our troops. But in 1973, the tree was a messenger of forgiveness and lasting love.

Chinese New Year is marked by hanging red envelopes on the branches of a tree. The higher the branch the wish is hung on, the greater the chance of it coming true. In Hong Kong, the banyan trees in Lam Tsuen in Fong Ma Po Village hold hundreds of wishes that have been tied to an orange then thrown up into the trees. Legend has it that the stronger the toss and the higher the wish lands, the better your chances of having your wish come true.

Peace trees around the world carry messages on their limbs written as affirmations and pleadings for peace. The requests come in peaceful quotes, poems, and fervent wishes for world peace.

In Vancouver, British Columbia, is a tree on the south end of the park on Jervis Street, between Burnaby and Harwood Streets. This tree has been the bearer of hundreds of messages and letters with inscriptions from passersby and visitors. It warms the heart to see trees full of wishes, hopes, and dreams.

Not all good intentions are rewarded, however. The Wishing Tree on the Hill of Tara in Ireland met a dreadful demise. So burdened by all the wishes hung on the tree, it cracked in half under the weight of the paper notes, materials, plastic, and assorted objects. Some Druids wondered if it might not have been the heavy nature of the wishes themselves that burdened the tree and caused its dramatic downfall.

The Tara Skryne preservation group tells us that wishing trees would have been long regarded by locals as portals to the fairy realm. "One would stand between the two trees and make a wish for something new to enter into your life, a new partner, job, etc. No tying of anything to the trees, no damage was done to them. What has been happening since approximately 2012 is that people are using these trees as if they were Rag Trees, or, as they are known in Scotland, as Clooties Trees, a totally different practice" (O'Shea 2019).

A rag tree, as a piece of information, is a tree on which rags are hung to help a sick person's illness go away. The rags are taken from a garment the ill person wore, thus establishing an energy connection between the rag, tree, and person needing healing. As the rag decays, the person's illness is thought to disappear. It also helps that the rag trees (traditionally hawthorns) are usually planted or found near holy healing wells. The roots absorb the water from the well, impart the healing to the tree, and the tree, in turn, heals the person as the rags fall off.

It seems wise then to consider the impact of our wishes on these beautiful trees. We should first ask the tree if it is willing to bear our wishes. Then, we should take care that we hang only lightweight, natural, and biodegradable products on the tree, making sure they won't choke or harm the tree in any way.

Perhaps the solution to having a compatible and sustainable relationship with a tree would be to follow what the Yogis teach. In Yogic teachings, your mind is the wishing tree of your life, and it contains the power to fulfill your desires. Use your mind to create a vision of what you want and leave the tree to be a living inspiration and natural beauty upon the earth, uncluttered by human additions.

Singing Trees

Have you ever heard a tree sing? They do, all the time, and the only thing we must do is listen. Our vast musical history speaks about trees in many ways. There are mentions of the songs in each tree and the way they speak; the whispering of pines, the rustling of leaves in a summer breeze, falling branches, the sharp snap of a branch breaking, crisp and crackling leaves, and the steady hum of tree camaraderie that vibrates through a forest. Add to that the fluttering and flapping of wings, the buzzing of bees, and the scurrying about of creatures large and small. Now we have a symphony.

Many composers and artists have always known or suspected that trees talk, even if they have no identifiable language. The redwood trees have been recorded talking to each other through the elaborate network of their roots systems. They communicate to other trees what they need, and sister trees gladly supply it. They have a warning system and a recovery system, all neatly tucked underground.

The cottonwood tree has darling little flat-stemmed leaves, and when the wind blows, they shimmer and rustle in the breeze. The leaves of the aspen quake in a breeze. The poplars have morphed over time to grow flat petioles that allow them to twitter in the winds.

What symphonies exist in your backyard? In the neighbor's garden? In the park? We are surrounded by trees that dance, sing, and play the symphonies of nature. We all have a front-row seat to the greatest concert on Earth, and all we have to do is listen.

Wands

A wand made from a tree is a wonderful, magical item to have. Some believe that making a wand from your favorite tree—the one you have connected to the most—is the best way to go, vibrationally speaking. Others maintain procuring a wand, making or buying it, from your birth month tree (Chapter Four) is more powerful. Others say, find the qualities of the tree you like the most and find a wand from that tree. Only you will know which wand is best for you.

I am always asked if purchasing a wand made by someone else is okay or if it is best to make your own wand. I always tell them, you'll know. You'll know what is best for the work you do, the life you lead, and whether you have any wood-carving skills. Many beautiful wands are available on the internet made by artisans who know what they are doing. There are wands to acquire and wands to dream of owning. Personally, I have an everyday wand and a dress-up wand. Don't ask me why; I just do.

When you are looking to find a wand, it will call to you. You may want to refresh your mind about each tree's qualities to select a wood that resonates with you. See that chart from the end of Chapter Nine and refresh your mind about what woods bring qualities with them to suit your purpose. I enjoy my wand made from hazel, my birth month tree.

You may even want to have a collection of wands. Ones that connect with the higher realms or earth energy. Do you want transformation, love attraction, protection? Figure out what magical qualities you want, and back into them with the qualities the woods offer you. (See the chart that follows.)

Wand shopping is one of my favorite things to do, and I have yet to know a person who didn't recognize *their* wand when they saw it. I like to remind the reticent that if they know how to order a pizza with their favorite toppings on it, they'll know how to pick their personal, magical wand.

People and trees have a lot in common. Since trees cannot speak for themselves and unselfishly give us many gifts, including health aides, which help us sustain our lives, isn't it fitting that we return the favor and look out for their safety and protection? I mean, isn't that what friends are for? We need the trees, and they need us. And it just so happens that right now trees do need our immediate help.

In 2018, Melbourne, Australia, assigned email addresses to 70,000 trees. This gesture created a fresh awareness of trees in the city, and people began writing them love letters.[3]

---

3   It is a heartwarming story, and you can read more about the phenomenon from Margaret Burin at: www.abc.net.au/news/2018-12-12/people-are-emailing-trees/10468964.

In the next chapter, we'll explore how trees need our assistance and exactly what we can do to help them live up to their full potential and longevity. If we have the right to life, liberty, and the pursuit of happiness, why shouldn't the trees?

Blessing

May the miracles of the trees enfold you.
May you find inspiration and comfort in their majesty.
May their branches lift your heart upward and keep you
suspended in a world of magic.
May you sense the deep, earthly connection in the mighty roots of
a tree and make them your own.
May your loftiest intentions bear fruit as easily and naturally as the bounty of a tree.
May you plant your wishes in the richest soil, and, like the seeds of a tree,
may they emerge effortlessly for you.
May the gentle breeze move through the branches of your mind and launch your
every dream, bringing you prosperity, healing, wisdom,
and love through the winds of change.

kac young 2021

Wand Wood	Specialties
Almond	Aaron's rod
Apple	Pierce veil of other worlds. Experienced magicians
Ash	Odin's spear
Cedar	Bless a sacred space
Cherry	Centered, grounding
Chestnut	Shaman wood
Dogwood	Wishes granted
Elder	Transformational magic
Elm	Fairy wands
Hawthorn	Fairy wands
Hemlock	Yin energy, radical transformation
Holly	Removes evil spirits
Hazel	Settle arguments, Druid wand
Mahogany	Conductor of vibration, natural magic
Maple	Bringer of gold
Mulberry	Ward off evil spirits
Myrtle	Love, long life
Olive	Peace, victory
Redwood	Sacred
Rowan	Fairy magic
Sassafras	Channeling
Willow	Enchantment
Yew	Otherworld connection

Chapter Twelve

Giving Back and Saving Ourselves and Our Magical Trees

After getting to know more about trees, the magical properties they have and understanding how we can work together to sustain and preserve life on many levels, the question that always comes up is, "What can we do to help save the trees and our planet?" One of the answers is planting and managing tree growth and harvesting according to a plan. To be frank, there are two sides to this controversial coin: the loggers who depend on cutting down trees and selling them for a living, and the conservationists who stand in the path of their chain saws to prevent them from culling the forests for profit.

Briefly, side one, the lumberjacks, say that removing trees from a forested area is a good thing because in doing so, according to Future Forest Consulting, there are six benefits of logging:

1. **Improves forest health**—When logged, the dead and diseased trees are harvested and removed, thereby preventing the spread of fungi or bacteria, damaging other parts of the tree and adjacent trees in the forest.

2. **Minimizes competition among the trees**—High densities of trees mean there will be more competition for a limited amount of nutrition between trees. Without logging and thinning of the density, various sections of forests will be compromised and undernourished.

3. **Provides necessary materials**—Logging is the main source of timber used for several human needs like providing construction materials for homes and businesses and furniture and fences.

4. **Safety**—When a tree is old, weak, or diseased, it becomes more prone to the destructive powers of wind and rain. When trees are allowed to grow unchecked, they can crush roofs of houses, power lines, and other buildings.

5. **Allows more ground area to flourish**—Lower densities of trees in the forest mean that there will be chances for more new growth in the forest. This allows for the growth of small plants and trees and adds to the soil's nutrient levels.

6. **Diminishes the risk of forest fire**—Since logging requires the cutting of trees, it is likely that any fire started by a natural cause will not spread as rapidly. In this way, the forest can be saved from any unexpected forest fires, and the lives of its wild habitats can also be saved (Corey 2021).

The opposite thinking from Side Two is that there are negative effects if logging is not carefully and meticulously managed.

1. **Habitat destruction**—Logging potentially removes habitats for birds and other wildlife that use trees for cover, nesting, or food. Owls, for example, prefer older trees with a larger diameter for nest cavities. If logging occurs along stream banks, the risk of flooding and erosion increases, as these trees help to anchor the soil in place. Large trucks used to transport felled trees travel on unimproved roads, which increases soil erosion and compounds its ill effects.

2. **Clear-cutting**—There is a distinct and important difference between forest management logging and clear-cut logging. Clear-cut logging means most or all trees in an area are uniformly cut down, leaving the land bare. Forest management can benefit forests, while clear-cutting destroys them. Clear-cutting is often practiced in tropical forests for harvesting wood and other plant products and opening space for development. Clear-cutting adversely affects wildlife by reducing habitat, and rare or threatened plant species are destroyed.

3. **Climate Change**—Logging can impact climate change by increasing the amount of free carbon dioxide in the atmosphere. Plant life stores carbon dioxide within its tissues. Deforestation often goes hand in hand with fire, which releases this stored carbon dioxide into the air, compounding the greenhouse gas effect. A 2009 study in the journal *Conservation Letters* found links between logging and fire vulnerability (Rogers 2019).

The debate continues. However, the sides are beginning to talk, each making more sense and starting a healing practice. The three main components of tree preservation are education, management, and responsibility. And herein lies the magic and healing the trees provide. We see a lot of this happening where loggers are being educated about what happens to the wildlife in a forested area where their trees are removed and they have no place to survive, breed, and evolve. When the loggers are educated, they leave behind wood piles where wildcats can gather, enough treetops still standing for the birds, and bark chards and decaying material for the insects. In Guyana, for example, where logging is a means of survival, there is a little church specifically for loggers. They preach kindness and balance for the earth.

The subject of illegal logging is a global problem, as is poaching. It happens in every country worldwide. One of the biggest threats to human rights and forest exploitation is harvesting the oil palm tree (*Elaeis guineensis*) and the cacao tree (*Theobroma cacao*). These harvesting industries use forced child labor and slavery to harvest these products. Indonesia and Malaysia account for 84 percent of the world's palm production. Palm oil is present in 50 percent of our food products and comes from forced labor, including children's labor. These children live in squalor with inadequate food and sanitation and are forced to work twelve to fourteen hours a day, hauling hundred-pound sacks of raw material through the forests on their backs. They are given heavy, dangerous saws and machetes to harvest the trees. Many are tortured and sexually abused.

Cacao plantations in Western Africa have been under fire for years and journalists are imprisoned who dared to expose the atrocities and slavery of the chocolate business. The majority of cacao comes from Western Africa, South America, and Asia. Child slavery is a norm and often achieved through kidnapping and false promises. The Fair-Trade Chocolate movement states that "Fair-trade chocolate is chocolate that is made with cacao beans from farmers who are paid a fair price for their crop, instead of the low-price set by the market" (Fair Trade Chocolate 2021). And still, this is a drop in the bucket of global child abuse for harvesting our sweet treats.

The actions we can take are to read the labels of the products we buy and make sure we are purchasing our foods and products as harm-free as they can be. I like to keep an eye on the luxuries I purchase, like chocolate, by checking the list of manufacturers who buy and sell with human rights at the forefront. Here is a link to check out: foodispower.org/chocolate-list.

This book would go on forever if we covered all the ways to sustain our planet, trees, animals, and water sources. I'll list a few places where you can begin your journey and further your knowledge if you want to know more.

ASPCA has an excellent website with humane animal information:

www.aspca.org/shopwithyourheart/consumer-resources/shop-your-heart-grocery-list

More about fair trade chocolate brands:

www.fairtradeamerica.org/shop-fairtrade/fairtrade-products/chocolate

Ethical Consumers is also a good information resource:

www.ethicalconsumer.org/food-drink/palm-oil-and-consumers

Fair Trade America is another good one:

www.fairtradeamerica.org/shop-fairtrade/fairtrade-products

Moving on to another way we can help and some cautions. For the past few years, I have chosen to remember people and their special occasions by having a tree planted in their honor. I may have made a few mistakes initially by buying the products of companies that are not ethically sound.

Michael Thau, the executive director of Plant-It 2020 since 1996 (a nonprofit tree-planting organization founded by the late John Denver), is also a fourth-degree Black Belt and has worked in sales and marketing positions before joining Plant-It 2020. He is dedicated to doing the right thing by the forests and not defrauding the public about it.

Michael states in a paper entitled "Tree Planting Scams and Deceptions" that some tree-planting companies "say they will 'plant-a-tree' and what they do is simply plop a tree seed in the ground, kick some dirt over the hole, and walk away" (Thau 2016). He claims they didn't plant a tree at all, only a potential tree in the form of a seed without proper upkeep or maintenance to grow it into a full and healthy tree, like what you believe you paid for. Here's more from his article:

1. First, tree-planting organizations should refer to planting a "tree seedling" (baby tree) and not a "tree seed."

2. Second, there are numerous things that need to be done in making sure that the seedling (if it is not a larger-sized tree) is planted properly. The seedling is usually grown in a seed bed until it is large, old, and strong enough to be transplanted into its final location.

3. Third, the physical mechanics of transplantation must be performed correctly.

4. Fourth, some seedlings must receive post-transplantation care such as watering, weed control, and protection from animals, like hungry deer, for some time. The percentage of trees that live for a certain amount of time after they are transplanted is called the "survival rate."

5. People in the industry who care more about quality than profitability look at these and other factors in determining if "planting-a-tree" is simply a marketing phrase to increase contributions or describing a philosophy where maximizing the long-term survival rate in a highly sustainable forest is the goal (Thau 2016).

Michael's article gave me a lot to think about. We can't believe all the marketing claims we read, and if we want to contribute to companies that plant and grow trees for us, we should rely on the companies he says are honorable and ethical. You can read more of his code of ethics at his web page: plantit2020.org. You can also buy a tree from them to be planted by volunteers worldwide. The list is amazing! Try plantit2020.org/locations.html.

I am grateful to Michael Thau for his work with trees and scam-less reforestation. He opened my eyes and now I can contribute in good conscience to the organizations that are effective earth-healers. Michael also recommends we patronize growforests.org, which will also put your money to use by ethically planting a tree for reforestation in a needed area.

Another of my favorite tree heroes is Diana Beresford-Kroger. She is a world-recognized author, medical biochemist, and botanist with a unique combination of Western scientific knowledge and the traditional concepts of the ancient world. According to her, ten trees are crucial to our planet's survival. Diana was orphaned in Ireland and was educated by elders who instructed her in the Brehon knowledge of plants and nature. She is a soul in the old ways of trees and spirits. It is worth your time to see her film, *Call of the Forest*. Here are the ten trees we need to save.

1. **The English Oak,** *Quercus robar*
This tree, also commonly referred to as the Irish oak or truffle oak, is native to Asia Minor (an area corresponding to the western two-thirds of Turkey), North Africa, the Caucasus (a geopolitical region at the border of Europe and Asia), and Europe.

2. **The Black Walnut,** *Juglans Nigra*
The Black Walnut is native to North America, where it is found in central and eastern USA and eastern Canada. It is renowned for its beautiful hardwood and nuts.

3. **Redwood,** *Sequoia semervirens*
The redwood is also referred to as the California redwood or coast redwood. It is an evergreen native to the Pacific Coast of North America.

4. **Atlas Cedar,** *Cedrus atlantica*
This cedar is often found in temperate gardens but is native to the Atlas Mountains of Morocco and Algeria in northern Africa.

5. **Baobab tree,** *Adansonia digitata*
Also referred to as the monkey bread or dead rat tree, the baobab can grow to a massive girth of twenty-eight meters. It is native to hot, dry savannahs of sub-Saharan Africa.

6. **Red mangrove,** *Rhizophora mangle*
The red mangrove likes to grow in swampy areas worldwide, in coastal and estuarine areas of the tropics and subtropics of the northern and the southern hemispheres.

7. **Teak,** *Tectona grandis*
Most famous for the beautiful furniture it is made into, teak is a deciduous hardwood tree native to India, Indonesia, Malaysia, Myanmar, northern Thailand, and northwestern Laos.

8. **Mountain ash eucalyptus,** *Eucalyptus regnans*
Also commonly called the swamp gum tree, *Eucalyptus regnans* can grow to over three hundred feet. It is native to southeastern Australia, Tasmania, and Victoria.

9. **Sugi,** *Cryptomeria japonica*
This is the national tree of its native Japan, where it is considered sacred and planted around shrines and temples. It is commonly called the Japanese cedar, but it is not a true cedar and is more closely related to the sequoia.

10. **Scots pine,** *Pinus sylvestris*
The Scots pine, also known as the scotch pine or scotch fir, is the most widespread conifer in the world. It is native to Europe and Asia, ranging from Scotland and Portugal in the west, to Siberia in the east, south to the Caucasus Mountains, and north to the Arctic Circle in Scandinavia (What Are the Ten Trees? 2021).

Please remember that the trees are native to different parts of the world, so if you decide to plant one, please make sure it is native to your area. Diana also has a nonprofit organization collecting seeds from trees around the world and starting a nursery of seedlings to replant where necessary.

Diana's website:

dianaberesford-kroeger.com

Call of the Forest website:

calloftheforest.ca

NCPR Podcast, *To Speak for the Trees*, Diana Beresford-Kroeger:

www.northcountrypublicradio.org/news/story/42767/20201201/a-global-bio-plan-that-s-as-simple-as-planting-a-tree

Trees are critical to us, not only for our breath and source of life, but also as our partners, symbols, and living beings that help us sustain our life on Earth. We must think about them in relationship to who we are, what we purchase, and how that purchase travels from tree to table. Were any persons, animals, or laws harmed by what we bought? Trees are a critical link and magical in our chain of life, and it must be our joy and mission to help them thrive as freely and safely as we do or wish to.

What I have learned about how we can take better care of trees has changed my life, and I have committed my life to buying only what is sustainable, harvested with kindness, and is suffering-free. It is the only way to be truly accountable to my beloved, magical, and sacred trees. I hope you'll buy trees for your special loved ones. It would mean a lot to the trees and the earth.

Get Involved!

Many community organizations are now planting trees in underserved neighborhoods to bring shade, health, beauty, and comfort back to the urban places that have experienced botanical neglect. According to Nature.org, planting trees in urban neighborhoods has proven to improve the residents' health by cooling the area's temperature, encouraging outdoor recreation, cleaning the air, and removing pollutants from the air, among many other things. New trees encourage economic development, enhance the beauty of the area, and raise property values, not to mention the spirit and the confidence of the people living there (Nature.org 2017).

The reference section at the back of the book has lists of local community organizations, available federal and state grants, and ways you can help repopulate the earth with the life-giving gift of trees.

Conclusion

Trees were here on earth long before humans showed up. When the first Homo Sapiens and Hominids arrived, they looked up at the sky and saw the trees waving in the breeze, painting their poetry in the air. What a sight that must have been and what a thrill it was to ultimately discover all of the bounty that trees have to offer humankind. The journey of discovery must have been filled with astonishment and delight for our early predecessors.

There are ancient cultures who came before us that sobbed when a tree was cut down because they were connected by their hearts to the world of trees. Our own Native Americans have had deep respect for tree spirits, long before Europeans invaded the land. Black Elk remind us,

> *"Some little root of every sacred tree still lives. Nourish it, that it may leaf and bloom and fill the air with singing birds." (Geihardt 1932)*

Historically, trees have gifted us with much more than shelter and coffee tables. They have given us medicines, a connection to the other worlds, and refuge from the toils of life. They are filled with inspiration, comfort, companionship, protection, music, and magic.

There is growing scientific proof that our future depends on trees. They can help us save our planet and reestablish equilibrium and eco-balance on earth. Here's what you can do to help:

+ Join a community of tree enthusiasts who are planting trees in urban and underserved areas to bring life and health back to that community.
+ Check out the list of organizations listed in the reference section and give some energy back to the world of trees.
+ Chapter Twelve provides links to inspirational people who are committed to trees and preserving them for future generations. Watch their films and connect.
+ Be part of the solution because you have acted and helped.

Chapter Twelve has links to inspirational people who are committed
to trees and preserving them for future generations. Watch their films,
be inspired ,and connect. You will feel like you are part of the solution
because you have reach out and helped.

I hope that this journey though the world of magical trees, their gifts and
descriptions, has given you joy and filled you with appreciation and perhaps
even adoration for the tree kingdom. I hope you will emerge from reading this
book with renewed faith, greater understanding, and a passion for helping the
trees live on long after we have spent our time on this beautiful planet. Get
inspired! Take action! Join your community to help save our precious trees! If
you don't help save them, they will be gone and so will our planet.

I send you my blessings, I share my love for the trees with you, and I wish you
bushels of beautiful hours discovering and experiencing the magic in trees and
becoming an activist to save the trees.

The call to action is *now*. Here's what *you* can do:

+ Go to this link and find out the key things you can do to save trees:
  reefoundation.org/10-things-you-can-do-to-save-forests/

+ Go to: growforests.org/ and plant a tree, save a tree, or help them with
  their mission to reforest.

+ Learn ways you can conserve to protect trees: greenwithless.com/
  save-trees/

Acknowledgments

I remember the magical moment when Brenda Knight, editor for Mango Publishing Group, asked me if I'd like to write a book about Magical Trees. I leaped at the opportunity. It became a book that I couldn't stop writing. I loved every moment of the process. I want to thank and credit Brenda for her wisdom and allowing me this excellent opportunity. She's the reason this book exists.

Thank you to the editorial staff, design staff, and marketing gang for their help getting this out to readers all over the world.

Deep gratitude to Marlene Morris for her encouragement, support, and dedicated proofing all my first drafts and her inspired content enhancement.

To Lisa Hagan, for always supporting my literary efforts and being the best agent anyone could ask for.

To my friends, Pamela Ventura, J. Randy Taraborrelli, Donna Wells, Lisa Tenzin-Dolma, Diane Wing, Victor Fuhrman, Dr. Paula Joyce, and the wonderful podcasters who interview me on their shows; thank you for believing in me and my work. I love you all so much.

Lastly, to the trees, for their bravery, courage, longevity, and the generous gifts they have given every human being who has ever walked on this planet. The more I learn about trees, the deeper my gratitude runs to our exquisite and natural Earth and all the living things on it. Thank you for giving me such amazing joy.

Appendix A

This Old Irish Tree List, as it has come to be known, not only provides us with a fascinating example of Brehon law in action but also gives us some insight into the nature of ancient Irish society and the role and importance of trees in the daily lives of our ancestors.

Airig Fedo
(Nobles)

- Dair/oak
- Coll/hazel
- Cuileann/holly
- Ibar/yew
- Uinnius/ash
- Ochtach/scots pine
- Aball/crab apple

Aithig Fedo
(Commoners)

- Fern/alder
- Sail/willow
- Scé/hawthorn
- Caorthann/rowan
- Beithe/birch
- Lem/elm
- Idath/cherry

Fodla Fedo
(Lower Divisions)

- Draigen/blackthorn
- Trom/elder
- Feoras/spindle
- Findcholl/whitebeam
- Caithne/arbutus
- Crithach/aspen
- Crann fir/juniper

Losa Fedo
(Bushes)

- Raith/bracken
- Rait/bog myrtle
- Aiten/furze
- Drís/bramble
- Fróech/heather
- Gilcach/broom
- Spín/wild rose

For further information, see the paper "Trees in Early Ireland" by Fergus Kelly, Augustine Henry Memorial Lecture, March 11, 1999, Royal Dublin Society, www.forestryfocus.ie/social-environmental-aspects/cultural-heritage/trees-and-folklore/brehon-laws.

Appendix B

Brehon Laws

Brehon Laws were the governing social rules that the Celts lived by. They originated in the seventh century and were the legal statutes written by lawyers called the Brehons and were followed until the British conquest of Ireland in the seventeenth century under Elizabeth I.

The laws were termed lewd and unreasonable by the Brits and supplanted with British Laws. But the Brehons preserved some of the manuscripts in volumes so we could look into their world. Mighty nice of them.

They were translated in the nineteenth century by Eugene O'Curry and John O'Donovan.

What was wonderful about Brehon laws was that women were equal. They could marry for a year and then divorce if they wanted to. They could own property and could function as judges too. The women were not "stuck" in marriage; they were free, once a year, to change their minds.

For more information and to read the full Brehon Laws, I suggest two links:

+ www.irishcentral.com/roots/history/equal-rights-for-women-in-ancient-ireland
+ www.irishcentral.com/roots/ireland-brehon-laws

References

List of Tree-Planting Enthusiasts to Help Underserved and Urban Communities

Re-Leaf: American Forests

www.americanforests.org/our-work/urban-forestry/all-places

Friends of Trees

www.friendsoftrees.org/blog/partnering-with-community-benefit-organizations-to-plant-trees-grow-community

Tree People

www.treepeople.org/2015/0568/california-releaf-real-conversations-working-disadvantaged-communities

Tree Canopy in Underserved Communities—USDA

www.fs.usda.gov/detail/r9/home/?cid=FSEPRD874761

Community Programs

www.publichealth.lacounty.gov/place/PLACE_Urban_Forest_Work.htm

Trees in Low-Income Neighborhoods

www.scientificamerican.com/article/trees-are-missing-in-low-income-neighborhoods

The Dirt

www.dirt.asla.org/2015/08/19/how-can-we-get-trees-to-those-who-need-them-the-most

Urban Forestry

www.biohabitats.com/newsletter/urban-forestry/non-profit-spotlight-alliance-for-community-trees

We Plant Trees

www.carbonforest.org/?gclid=CjwKCAjwruSHBhAtEiwA_
qCpprm4ftcHCO-3gtAxznkHiIU9mVes8aQT0P4r3_dT-
Fzb8qCWBt-wsxoCiW8QAvD_BwE

Grants for Tree Planting

www.californiareleaf.org/programs/grants

Federal Grants for Tree Planting

www.fs.usda.gov/working-with-us/grants

Essential Oils Extracted from Our Fifty Trees

Acacia
Acacia (Cassie) oil is used in bath and skincare products, folk medicine, perfumery, and massage. The flowers of the cassie plant have antiseptic and antibacterial properties.

Alder
Alder oil is available from some private distillers. However, the quality and purity of private distillation and extraction cannot be guaranteed. Ginger (*Zingiber officinale*) essential oil is compatible.

Almond
Almonds can be sweet or bitter, depending on the type of tree that produces them. Sweet almond is usually a carrier oil. Bitter almond does contain toxic chemicals.

Apple
There is no commercially available, steam-distilled apple fruit (pulp) essential oil or an apple blossom essential oil. Fragrance oils are available that are engineered to smell like apples or apple pie.

Ash
Ash oil is available from some private distillers. However, the quality and purity of private distillation and extraction cannot be guaranteed. Lilac (*Syringa vulgaris*) essential oil is compatible.

Aspen

Aspen oil is available from some private distillers. However, the quality and purity of private distillation and extraction cannot be guaranteed. Melissa (*Melissa officinalis L.*) is compatible.

Avocado

Some may refer to avocado oil as an essential oil, but that's not entirely accurate. Viscous and green-colored, avocado oil is considered a carrier oil.

Banyan

Banyan oil is available from some private distillers. However, the quality and purity of private distillation and extraction cannot be guaranteed.

Baobab

Baobab seed oil is cold-pressed from seeds for various uses, from cooking to hair care to skincare. It is rich in omega-3 fatty acids and other fats.

Beech

Beech nut essential oil is available. However, the quality and purity of private distillation and extraction cannot be guaranteed.

Birch

Several components make up the birch essential oil, salicylic acid, methyl salicylates, butylene, and betulinal. Birch oil has a fresh, minty aroma, a sharp and familiar fragrance that is soothing and calming.

Boswellia

Frankincense, also known as olibanum, is made from the resin of the Boswellia tree. This tree typically grows in the dry, mountainous regions of India, Africa, and the Middle East.

Cedar

Cedarwood essential oil is a substance derived from the needles, leaves, bark, and berries of cedar trees. Various cedar trees are found around the world. Some trees referred to as cedars are juniper trees.

Cherry
Cherry essential oil has a rich, ripe, fruity aroma, warmth, and happiness. It is used in aromatherapy for skin care, hair care, massage, bathing, making perfumes, soaps, scented candles, and more.

Chestnut
Chestnut oil is obtained from the kernel of the chestnut. Chestnut is also known as horse chestnut. It is native to the northern hemisphere. Horse chestnut is lethal if consumed raw.

Coconut
Coconut oil is pressed from the meat of the coconut. Oil pressed from fresh, unprocessed coconut "meat" is called "virgin." "Refined" coconut oil is made from dried coconut meat, and "fractionated" means it has been heated beyond its melting point. Fractionation keeps the oil liquid.

Coffee
Coffee blossom essential oil is extracted from the pillowy white blossoms of the coffee plant. It is antiseptic, anti-inflammatory, and astringent.

Cottonwood
Cottonwood is rich in balsamic resin, which acts as a topical anti-inflammatory. It is also used as an analgesic and anti-inflammatory herbal oil.

Cypress
Cypress oil is an essential oil made from the cypress tree's twigs, stems, and leaves. Cypress oil has many health benefits, including antibacterial, antimicrobial, and antifungal properties.

Dogwood
Dogwood essential oil is available. However, the quality and purity of private distillation and extraction cannot be guaranteed.

Elder
Elderflower essential oil comes from a plant and not a tree.

Elm

Elm tree essential oil is available. However, the quality and purity of private distillation and extraction cannot be guaranteed.

Eucalyptus

Steam-distilled from the eucalyptus tree, it has the properties of eucalyptol and alpha-terpineol, which aid with respiratory conditions. There are many varieties of eucalypts; choose the oil from the varietal that suits your needs.

Fig

Fig oil is available as a fig fragrance oil. However, the quality and purity of private distillation and extraction cannot be guaranteed.

Fir

Several fir needle oils are available: Balsam, Douglas, Siberian, Grand. Choose the ones with the properties you desire.

Ginkgo

Gingko Biloba essential oil is available. However, the quality and purity of private distillation and extraction cannot be guaranteed.

Hazel *Corylus avellana*

Hazelnut oil is a carrier oil. It has a high concentration of omega-9 and vitamin E and moisturizes, protects, and helps maintain the skin's elasticity and suppleness.

Hemlock

Hemlock essential oil is steam-distilled from conifer trees and is not related to the poisonous hemlock plant (a member of the parsley family). It is used to support the breath, chest, and throat for colds, congestion, and sore throats.

Hawthorn

Hawthorn berry essential oil is available and is a rich source of polyphenols.

Holly

Holly berry essential oil is available. However, the quality and purity of private distillation and extraction cannot be guaranteed.

Jacaranda
Jacaranda essential oil is available and has microbial properties. It has been used for treating bacterial infections, gonorrhea, syphilis, and leukemia.

Juniper
Juniper essential oil is made from juniper berries. The oil is inhaled to treat bronchitis and numb pain.

Lemon
Lemon essential oil is cold-pressed from the peels of lemon fruit. It has antibacterial, antifungal, astringent, and antimicrobial properties.

Linden
Linden blossom essential oil is used in perfumes for its scent. It has been used to induce sweating for alleviating feverish colds and infections and reducing nasal congestion, sore throat, and cough.

Mahogany
Mahogany oil is used in wood-staining and beard-grooming. It also comes as a fragrance oil. However, the quality and purity of private distillation and extraction cannot be guaranteed.

Magnolia
Magnolia oil is steam-distilled from the sturdy petals of the magnolia flower. Like lavender and bergamot, magnolia is primarily linalool, which may help with feelings of stress or anxiousness and can be relaxing.

Maple
Maple essential oil is available, as is maple pecan, maple teak, and more. However, the quality and purity of private distillation and extraction cannot be guaranteed.

Mulberry
Mulberry essential oil is primarily used as a fragrance oil. Any other mulberry oil cannot be guaranteed quality and purity due to private distillation and extraction.

Myrtle

Myrtle essential oil is distilled from the branch of the myrtle tree. It has a sweet, herbal, camphor-like aroma, which can open the breath and clear the head.

Neem

Neem essential oil is a healing oil. It is also used for gardening as an insect repellant and carrier oil. Neem oil is rich in fatty acids, such as palmitic, linoleic, and oleic acids, which help support healthy skin.

Oak

The closest you'll get to oak essential oil is oak moss essential oil. Oak moss oil is a solvent extracted from the lichen that grows on oak trees. It has a green, woody, slightly fruity, earthy scent.

Olive

Olive oil can be used as a skin emollient and acne preventative and is softening and anti-aging.

Orange

Orange essential oil can be used for mood lifting, stress reduction, and as a room freshener. Properties include antimicrobial, analgesic, and anti-anxiety.

Palm

Red palm oil is vibrant in reddish-orange color packed with carotene and vitamins A and E! It is used as a hair moisturizer and skin moisturizer. Care should be taken because the color may stain clothing.

Pine

Pine needle oil is readily available. It is steam-distilled from pine needles and has a brilliant aroma straight from the forest. It helps with respiration and congestion.

Redwood

Redwood needle essential oil is available. However, the quality and purity of private distillation and extraction cannot be guaranteed.

Rowan

Berries and the bark are decocted but no known essential oil exists other than some for magical purposes.

Sassafras

Sassafras oil is available in essential oil and fragrance oil. However, the quality and purity of private distillation and extraction cannot be guaranteed.

Willow

White willow bark oil is available. However, the quality and purity of private distillation and extraction cannot be guaranteed.

Yew

Yew oil is available. However, the quality and purity of private distillation and extraction cannot be guaranteed.

Safety Notes about Essential Oils

Always take precautions to dilute pure essential oils with a carrier oil before applying to skin. Follow proper guidelines for using with the elderly, children, or adults. Consult with a doctor if you are pregnant. If you experience any adverse effects, promptly remove the oil from the skin with a neutral oil like olive or almond oil and call your doctor.

It is advisable when purchasing essential oils that you do so from a reputable distributor and look for organic, 100 percent pure, or wildcrafted on the label. Oils that are not marked accordingly may have been grown with pesticides or chemicals or contain toxic matter. Some are also diluted with less expensive oils.

Kac Young, PhD, is the author of two books on essential oils: *Essential Oils for Beginners* and *The Healing Art of Essential Oils*.

Crystals and Gemstones Compatible with Our Fifty Trees

Acacia	Citrine	Creativity, intuition, self-esteem, confidence, abundance, counteracts negativity.
Alder	Yellow calcite	Self-confidence, hope, personal motivation.
Almond	Agate	Enhances mental function, perception, analytical abilities, concentration.
Apple	Red jasper	Courage, self-confidence, emotional protection, dream recollection, sexual vibrancy.
Ash	Chrysoprase	Equalizes emotional balance, heals a broken heart, relaxing, helps to prevent nightmares.
Aspen	Golden topaz	Divine light, ancient wisdom, understanding, connection to ancestors.
Avocado	Jade	Protection from harm, promotes harmony, brings good luck and friendship.
Banyan	Aventurine	Prosperity, longevity, leadership, compassion, perseverance.
Baobab	Smoky topaz	Reduces fear, promotes positivity, relieves stress and anxiety.
Beech	Silver jasper	Strength, stability, grounding, insight.
Birch	Black tourmaline	Absorbs negativity, grounding, healing.
Boswellia	Tiger's eye	Protection, stabilizes, enhances psychic skills.
Cedar	Bronzite	Courage, unsettled emotions, power to move forward, protection.

Cherry	Ruby Rose quartz	Passion, vitality, opens the heart, tantric energy. Unconditional love, relationship healing.
Chestnut	Brown sea jasper	Responsibility, nurturing, healing of lower chakras.
Coconut	Moonstone	Intuition, psychic abilities, compassion, clairvoyance.
Coffee	Brown tourmaline	Gentle soothing of all emotions, relaxation for matters of the heart.
Cottonwood	Polished selenite	Peace, calm, mental clarity, connection with the higher realms.
Cypress	Green jade	Peace, calm, mental clarity, connection with the higher realms.
Dogwood	Polished snow quartz	Clarity, innocence, connecting with higher self.
Elder	Tree agate	Inner stability, balance, even distribution.
Elm	Chrysoprase	Equalizes emotional balance, heals a broken heart, relaxing, helps to prevent nightmares.
Eucalyptus	Australian chrysoprase	Happiness, enterprise, prudence.
Fig	Ruby fuchsite Moonstone	Courage, strength, emotional support, intuition, psychic abilities, compassion, clairvoyance.
Fir	Green sea jasper	Balance, healing, heart-opening.
Ginkgo	Yellow jade	Energetic, stimulating, brings joy and happiness.
Hawthorn	Poppy jasper	Courage, strength, will power, heals heartbreak.
Hazel	Brown labradorite	Spiritual expansion, higher levels of mind.
Hemlock	Charoite	Purifying, selflessness, compassion.

Holly	Red jasper	Grounding, justice, peace, insight.
Jacaranda	Purple tourmaline	Purification, achievement, affability.
Juniper	Green kyanite	High energy channel, attunement, meditation, psychic conductor.
Lemon	Citrine	Creativity, intuition, self-esteem, confidence, abundance, counteracts negativity.
Linden	Yellow calcite	Self-confidence, hope, clearing old patterns.
Mahogany	Polished stromatolite	Transformation, dissolves blockages, healing.
Magnolia	Scolecite	Intuition, inner vision, inner peace, transformation, enlightenment.
Maple	Red sardonyx	Purification, protection, bravery, perception.
Mulberry	Dark sugalite	Finding purpose, physical healing, protection.
Myrtle	White jade	Composure, calm, centering.
Neem	Apple green jasper	Internal harmony, positivity, balancing.
Oak	Carnelian	Courage, endurance, energy, leadership, motivation.
Olive	Fluorite	Intuition, connection to spirit, harmonizing.
Orange	Orange calcite	Higher consciousness, clears negativity, aids spiritual growth.
Palm	Rhyolite	Change, variety, progress, balance.
Pine	Green variscite	Intellect, grounding, wealth.
Redwood	Unakite	Vision, balance, grounding.
Rowan	Dragon's bloodstone	Strength, courage, confidence, endurance, focus.

Sassafras	Baltic amber	Spontaneity, wisdom, balance, self-expression, patience.
Willow	Turquoise	Shaman's Stone for protection, balance, intuition, friendship.
Yew	Clear quartz	Universal healer, spiritual growth, focus.

Works Cited

2021. "Acacia Wood USA." *Acacia Wood USA.* Feb 10. acaciawoodusa.com/ pages/what-is-acacia-wood/.

Adams, Cecil. 2006. "The Straight Dope Forbidden Fuit in the Garden of Eden." *The Straight Dope.* Nov 24. www.straightdope.com/21343798/ was-the-forbidden-fruit-in-the-garden-of-eden-an-apple.

2021. "American Conifer Society." *Juniperus Genus juniper.* 3 6. conifersociety.org/conifers/juniperus-1/?gclid=CjwKCAi AkJKCBhAyEiwAKQBCkmFeo2B27bWWVDTJZGe_ X5cwvezQXuFQScNSYVvw3yVEnDG6KCxQsRoCvvMQAvD_BwE.

2021. "Britannica.com." *Britannica.com/elm-tree.* 3 3. www.britannica.com/ plant/elm-tree.

2021. "Buried Mirror Yaxche Tree." *Buried Mirror.* Feb 22. www buriedmirror.com/yaxche.htm.

Caro, Tina. 2021. "Pine Tree Symbolism." *Magickalspot.* Mar 11. magickalspot.com/pine-tree-symbolism-meaning/.

Chen, Amy. 2013. "GingkoBilobaTheEndangered RedPlantblogspot." Mar 12. ginkgobilobatheendangeredplant.blogspot.com/.

Cohn, Roger. 2013. "Yale Environment 360." *Yale Environment 360.* May 1. e360.yale.edu/features/peter_crane_history_of_ginkgo_earths_ oldest_tree.

corey. 2021. "Six Benefits of Logging Forests." *Future Forest Consulting Inc.* 2 22. www.futureforestinc.com/six-benefits-of-logging-forests/.

Devaney, Erik. 2010. "Garden Guides, uses of elm tree." *GardenGuides.com.* Dec 16. www.gardenguides.com/12439086-the-uses-of-elm-trees.html.

2021. "Eden Project—Yew." *Eden Project.* 3 12. www.edenproject.com/learn/ for-everyone/plant-profiles/yew.

2021. "Fair Trade Chocolate." *Lake Champlain Chocolates.* Feb 22. www. lakechamplainchocolates.com/fair-trade-chocolate.

2013. "FineDiningLovers.com." 3 19. www.finedininglovers.com/article/
chestnuts-z-26-things-about-chestnuts.

2021. *Forestry Focus.* 2 20. www.forestryfocus.ie/social-environmental-
aspects/cultural-heritage/trees-and-folklore/brehon-laws/.

2011. "Frankincense and the Magi's Endangered Tree." *Garden Design.* www.
gardendesign.com/holiday/frankincense.html.

Fraser, Jack. 2017. "How The Human Body Creates Electromagnetic Fields."
Forbes. Nov 3. www.forbes.com/sites/quora/2017/11/03/how-the-
human-body-creates-electromagnetic-fields/?sh=7102debf56ea.

Geihardt, Black Elk and John G. 1932. "Black Elk (1863–1950) and John G.
Geihardt (1881–1973)." *Black Elk Speaks (1932).* Accessed 3 22, 2021.
facweb.st-agnes.org/home/pmcfarlin/html/BlackElktext.html.

Gerhard, Larry. 2019. "Ancient Tree with Record of Earth's Magnetic Field
Reversal in Its Rings Discovered." *Industry Tap.* Jul 29. www.industrytap.
com/ancient-tree-with-record-of-earths-magnetic-field-reversal-in-its-
rings-discovered/49559.

Grieve, Mrs. M. 2021. "Botanical." *Botanical. com.* 3 5. www.botanical.com/
botanical/mgmh/h/holly-28.html.

Grindstaff, Thomma Lyn. 2021. "Interesting Facts About Weeping Willow
Trees." *Love to Know Home and Garden.* 3 12. garden.lovetoknow.com/
wiki/Weeping_Willow_Tree_Facts.

Gruben, Michelle. 2017. *Grove and Grotto, Magickal Properties of Birch.* Aug 1.
www.groveandgrotto.com/blogs/articles/magickal-properties-of-birch.

Guthrie, Latisha. 2014. "Amulet Magazine." *www.Amulet Magazine.com.* Feb
18. www.amuletmagazine.com/2014/02/how-the-cottonwood-got-its-
star-latisha-guthrie/.

Haritan, Adam. 2021. "Wild Foodism." *Health Benefits of Drinking Maple Sap.*
3 10. wildfoodism.com/2015/02/24/the-health-benefits-of-drinking-
maple-tree-sap.

2021. *Home Stratosphere.* Feb 21. www.homestratosphere.com/
types-of-trees/.

II, Thomas Maugh. 2009. *Los Angeles Times Archives*. Dec 22. www.latimes. com/archives/la-xpm-2009-dec-22-la-sci-oak23-2009dec23-story.html.

2021. "Kiddle." *Rowan Facts for Kids*. Feb 15. kids.kiddle.co/Rowan.

Kornevall, Andreas. 2017. "The World Tree Yggdrasil." *Medium.com*. Dec 9. medium.com/@andreaskornevall/the-world-tree-yggdrasill-7b120b75a72a.

Leonard, David Bruce. 2021. "Pioneer Thinking." *Coffee as an Herbal Medicine*. 3 12. pioneerthinking.com/coffee-as-an-herbal-medicine/.

Leschmann, Theresa. 2017. "Gardening Guides." *GardeningGuides.com*. Sep 21. www.gardenguides.com/119125-interesting-cypress-trees.html.

2010. *Librate.com Banyan Tree Benefits*. Jul 1. www.lybrate.com/topic/banyan-tree-benefits.

2021. "Life Extension." *Lie Extension Science and Reasearch*. 1 16. www.lifeextension.com/magazine/2013/6/anti-inflammatory-properties of tart-cherry.

Lloyd, Ellen. 2019. "Ancient Pages." *Ancient Pages.com*. Feb 11. www.ancientpages.com/2019/02/11/irminsul-mysterious-sacred-symbol-of-the-saxons-is-it-linked-to-yggdrasil-and-god-odin/.

Mehrotra, Radhika. 2017. "Speaking Tree.IN." *Speaking Tree*. May 7. www.speakingtree.in/blog/secret-of-bodhi-tree-the-actual-tree-was-hacked-down-by-this-cruel-ruler-what-followed-will-amaze-you.

Murphy, Lydia. 2016. "Half of the world's Magnolia are threatened with extinction." *Global Trees Campaign*. Mar 18. globaltrees.org/news-blog/half-of-the-worlds-magnolias-are-threatened-with-extinction/.

Nagar, Muralilal. 2021. "Mopsoace.umsystem." *Ashvattha Sri Krishan pdf*. Feb 22. mospace.umsystem.edu/xmlui/bitstream/handle/10355/15530/AshvatthaShriKrishna.pdf;sequence=1.

2017. "Nature.org." *www.nature.org/content/dam/tnc/nature/en/documents/Public_Health_Benefits_Urban_Trees_FINAL.pdf*. Accessed 5 22, 2021. www.nature.org/content/dam/tnc/nature/en/documents/Public_Health_Benefits_Urban_Trees_FINAL.pdf.

2021. "Notes: Eej Mod Mother Tree." *Japanesemythology.wordpress.com/eej-mod-the-mother-tree-of-the-mongolians/*. Feb 20. japanesemythology. wordpress.com/eej-mod-the-mother-tree-of-the-mongolians/.

Nykos. 2021. "Rowan Tree Magical Properties." *The Witch and Wand.* Jan 21. www.thewitchandwand.com/post/rowan-wood-magical-properties.

2021. "Olivida Blog." *Olivida.* 3 12. www.oliviadaolive.com/facts-about-olive-tree/.

O'Shea, Kerry. 2019. "Irish Central News Wishing Tree Hill of Tara." *Irish Central News.* Jul 15. www.irishcentral.com/news/wishing-tree-hill-of-tara.

2021. "Paghat.com." *Myths and Legends of the Holly Tree.* 3 6. paghat.com/hollymythology.html.

Removers, Mold. 2021. "Wood Turning Pens JAcaranda." *Wood Turning Pens.* 3 10. www.woodturningpens.com/jacaranda/.

Robbins, Ocean. 2019. "Food Revolution Network Blog Almonds." *Food Revolution Network.* Jun 7. foodrevolution.org/blog/almonds-sustainability/.

Rogers, Chris Dinesen. 2019. "Logging and its effect on the ecosystem." *Sciencing.com.* Nov 22. sciencing.com/the-effects-of-cutting-down-trees-on-the-ecosystem-12000334.html.

Russel, Sean. 2021. "What is Palm Tree Wood Used For?" *Hunker.* 3 10. www.hunker.com/12567612/what-is-palm-tree-wood-used-for.

Sanders, Robert. 2011. "If plants generate magnetic fields, they're not sayin'." *Berkeley News.* Apr 7. news.berkeley.edu/2011/04/07/if-plants-generate-magnetic-fields-they%E2%80%99re-not-sayin%E2%80%99/.

2020. *Soft Schools.* Dec 1. www.softschools.com/facts/plants/birch_tree_facts/593/.

Sosa, Severina. 2020. "The FAces of the Goddess." *Witchology Magazine.* Jul 1. medium.com/witchology-magazine/the-faces-of-the-goddess-82dcf0fe93d1.

Spengler, Teo. 2021. "Orange Tree Facts." *Hunker.* 3 10. www.hunker.com/13428683/varieties-of-oranges.

Sproul, Barbara C. 1979. *Primal Myths*. HarperOne HarperCollinsPublishers.

Stancil, Joanna Mounce. 2019. "The Power of One Tree—The Very Air We Breathe." *USDA Gov Media*. Jun 3. www.usda.gov/media/blog/2015/03/17/power-one-tree-very-air-we-breathe.

2019. "Surviving Mexico." *Surviving Mexico Adventures and Disasters*. May 21. survivingmexico.com/tag/medicinal-use-of-jacaranda/.

Thau, Michael. 2016. "Plant It 2020." *Plant it 2020*. 7 21. fliphtml5.com/igjf/tikj/basic.

2021. "The Fact Site. Oak Tree Facts." *The Fact Site*. 3 12. www.thefactsite.com/oak-tree-facts/.

2021. "The Goddess Tree, Oak." *The Goddess Tree*. 3 10. www.thegoddesstree.com/trees/Oak.htm.

2021. "The Herbal Resource." *Holly-Uses and Medicinal Applications*. Mar 6. www.herbal-supplement-resource.com/holly-herb-benefits.html

1992. "The National Academies Sciences Engineering Medicine." *The National Academies Press. Neem A Tree for Solving Global Problems*. www.nap.edu/read/1924/chapter/11.

2021. "Thorogood Timber Merchant." *Thorogood Timber Merchant*. Feb 21. www.thorogood.co.uk/the-irokos-indomitable-role-in-african-culture/.

2007. "Top Verses of the Bible/Deuteronomy." *Top Verses of The Bible*. Mar 4. www.t.topverses.com/Bible/Deuteronomy/8/8.

Trufaith7. Apr. "Owlcation Pine Trees: Meanings and Culture of the Great Evergreen." *Owlcation*. 2020 23. owlcation.com/social-sciences/pine-trees#.

Usvat, Liliana. 2014. "Palm tree Medicinal Uses, History, Planting Tips, Soil Needs, Symbolism." *Liliana Usvat—Reforestation and Medicinal Use of the Trees*. Mar 4. lilianausvat.blogspot.com/2014/03/palm-tree-medicinal-uses-history.html.

Watts, Jonathan. 2019. "More than half of native European trees face extinction, warns study." *The Guardian*. Sep 27. www.theguardian.com/environment/2019/sep/27/more-than-half-of-native-european-trees-face-extinction-warns-study.

Wauters, Laurel. 2021. "Coffee—Balance." *Tree Spirit Wisdom*. 3 13. treespiritwisdom.com/tree-spirit-wisdom/coffee-tree-symbolism/.

2021. "What Are the Ten Trees?" *Call of the Forest*. 3 12. calloftheforest.ca/what-are-the-10-trees/.

2021. "Wonders of Neem." *Nature Neem*. 3 9. natureneem.com/en/wonders-of-neem.

2021. "Woodland Trust." *Ancient Tree Inventory*. 2 28. ati.woodlandtrust.org.uk/how-to-record/species-guides/beech/.

2020. "WWF." * *Things to Know About Palm Trees*. Jan 17. www.wwf.org.uk/updates/8-things-know-about-palm-oil.

Additional Resources

Wooden Ogham Acorns: Casey "Beast" Clark. BeastsCuriosities.com or see Etsy for Ogham Acorns.

www.tesswhitehurst.com/the-magical-and-metaphysical-properties-of-trees/

www.dragonoak.com/Magical-Wood-Properties.html

www.witchesofthecraft.com/2012/01/11/tree-magick-earth-magick

www.witcheslore.com/bookofshadows/herbology/plant-and-herb-magic-2/1174/

www.witchcraftandwitches.com/flower-tree-meanings/oak-tree-meaning-with-healing-metaphysical-magical-properties/?web_1&wdLOR=c286131FC-AFD7-4BC9-8976-F376392B256C

www.aliisaacstoryteller.com/post/ogham-the-secret-code-of-our-ancestors

www.ancient.eu/Ogham

www.ultimatehistoryproject.com/irish-letters-ogham-written-in-stone.html

www.forestryfocus.ie/social-environmental-aspects/cultural-heritage/trees-and-folklore/ogham

www.stairnaheireann.net/2017/01/12/celtic-mythology-five-sacred-guardian-trees-of-ireland/

www.cpp.edu/~jcclark/ogham/ogh-tree.html

www.cathyskipper.wordpress.com/2017/04/11/trees-as-spiritual-teachers/

www.irishcentral.com/roots/ireland-brehon-laws

www.oldest.org/nature/trees/

www.psy-minds.com/world-tree-symbol/

www.ancient-origins.net/myths-legends-europe/norse-legend-world-tree-yggdrasil-002680

www.users.skynet.be/lotus/tree/chinese0-en.htm

www.gardeningknowhow.com/ornamental/trees/acacia/acacia-tree-types.htm

www.fs.fed.us/research/urban-webinars/ash-tree-conservation-resistance-breeding.php

www.treesforlife.org.uk/into-the-forest/trees-plants-animals/trees/aspen/aspen-project/

www.speakingofwitchwands.net/2013/11/19/the-magickal-avocado-tree/

www.curejoy.com/content/avocado-origin/

www.eatweeds.co.uk/beech-fagus-sylvatica

www.lifeextension.com/magazine/2013/6/anti-inflammatory-properties-of-tart-cherry

www.finedininglovers.com/article/chestnuts-z-26-things-about-chestnuts

www.softschools.com/facts/plants/coconut_tree_facts/560/

www.gardenguides.com/119125-interesting-cypress-trees.html

www.thetreecenter.com/dogwood-tree-facts/

www.hhhistory.com/2018/03/the-legend-history-of-dogwood-tree.html

www.treespiritwisdom.com/tree-spirit-wisdom/dogwood-tree-symbolism/

www.botanical.com/botanical/mgmh/e/elder-04.html

www.gardenguides.com/12439086-the-uses-of-elm-trees.html

www.coniferousforest.com/plants-trees/fir

www.controverscial.com/In%20Worship%20of%20Trees%20-%20Hawthorn.htm

www.baobabfoundation.co.za

www.speakingofwitchwands.net/2020/01/28/the-magickal-baobab-tree/

www.e360.yale.edu/features/peter_crane_history_of_ginkgo_earths_oldest_tree

www.lifeofwaya.com/tag/magical-properties-of-ginko/

www.nhpbs.org/wild/poisonhemlock.asp

www.thespruce.com/canadian-hemlock-trees-2132061

www.druidgarden.wordpress.com/2014/01/02/sacred-tree-profile-eastern-hemlock-tsuga-canadensis-magic-mythology-and-qualities/

www.botanical.com/botanical/mgmh/h/holly-28.html

www.woodworkingnetwork.com/wood/wood-month/holly-beautiful-toxic

www.webmd.com/vitamins/ai/ingredientmono-724/juniper

www.conifersociety.org/conifers/juniperus-1/?gclid=CjwKCAi
AkJKCBhAyEiwAKQBCkmFeo2B27bWWVDTJZGe_
X5cwvezQXuFQScNSYVvw3yVEnDG6KCxQsRoCvvMQAvD_BwE

www.ehtrust.org/electromagnetic-fields-impact-tree-plant-growth/

www.industrytap.com/ancient-tree-with-record-of-earths-magnetic-field-reversal-in-its-rings-discovered/49559

www.atozflowers.com/flower/jacaranda

www.lilianausvat.blogspot.com/2014/10/jacaranda-tree-medicinal-uses.html

www.spiritualunite.com/articles/lemon-spiritual-meaning/

www.greekalicious.nyc/greekalicious-2/wisdom-lemons/

www.healthline.com/nutrition/6-lemon-health-benefits#TOC_
TITLE_HDR_4

www.hunker.com/13424424/facts-about-the-alder-tree

www.hunker.com/12000383/do-citrus-trees-have-good-wood

www.sunset.com/home-garden/edible-gardening/citrus-greening-disease-wasp-savior

www.thegoddesstree.com/trees/Birch.htm

www.nimvo.com/everything-you-need-to-know-about-the-linden-tree.

www.speakingofwitchwands.net/2018/09/04/the-magickal-linden-treeor-lime-tree/

www.gardeningknowhow.com/ornamental/trees/mahogany/information-on-mahogany-trees.htm

www.forestgeneration.com/mahogany.html

www.herbpathy.com/Uses-and-Benefits-of-Borneo-Mahogany-Oil-Cid10851

www.wicca.com/celtic/celtic-deities.html

www.softschools.com/facts/plants/mulberry_facts/1397/

www.justfunfacts.com/interesting-facts-about-mulberries/

www.ayurvedicindia.info/neem-tree

www.nap.edu/read/1924/chapter/11

www.natureneem.com/en/wonders-of-neem

www.tamilandvedas.com/2017/06/11/significance-of-neem-tree-in-hinduism-post-no-3992/

www.witchipedia.com/book-of-shadows/herblore/oak/

www.verywellhealth.com/herbal-supplements-benefits-risks-side-effects-interactions-5202322

www.hunker.com/13428683/varieties-of-oranges

www.verywellhealth.com/herbal-supplements-benefits-risks-side-effects-interactions-5202322

www.webmd.com/food-recipes/health-benefits-oranges

www.thespruce.com/fascinating-facts-about-palm-trees-2736717

www.treehugger.com/surprising-facts-about-palm-trees-4864291

www.justfunfacts.com/interesting-facts-about-pine-trees/

www.joybileefarm.com/pine-needle-tea/

www.owlcation.com/social-sciences/pine-trees

www.magickalspot.com/pine-tree-symbolism-meaning/

www.hilltromper.com/article/ten-amazing-facts-about-redwoods

www.thegoddesstree.com/trees/RedWood.htm

www.delishably.com/sauces-preserves/rowan-jelly-recipe

www.kids.kiddle.co/Rowan

www.thewitchandwand.com/post/rowan-wood-magical-properties

www.alltreatment.com/destruction-of-the-sassafras-tree/?__cf_chl_
rt_tk=e8LTMrk_lNxGauNy_qqSzn19fiyUn_.QvFxVgAae7.U-
1637705263-0-gaNycGzNCJE

www.balconygardenweb.com/sassafras-tree-facts/

www.thefreelibrary.com/
Magic+tree:+sassafras+was+once+believed+to+be+capable+of+warding
+off...-a0150988142

www.tapatalk.com/groups/thegoddesswithinapaganplaceforwomen/
sassafras-lore-t6865.html

www.softschools.com/facts/plants/willow_tree_facts/555/

www.edenproject.com/learn/for-everyone/plant-profiles/yew

www.thegoddesstree.com/trees/Yew.htm

www.homestratosphere.com/types-of-trees/

www.gardenguides.com/12460529-the-life-cycle-of-a-magnolia-tree.html

www.softschools.com/facts/plants/magnolia_tree_facts/599/

www.globaltrees.org/news-blog/half-of-the-worlds-magnolias-are-
threatened-with-extinction/

www.magickalspot.com/magnolia-tree-meaning-symbolism/

www.speakingofwitchwands.net/2020/03/03/the-magickal-boswellia-tree-
or-the-frankincense-tree/

www.aromatics.com/blogs/wellness/what-is-frankincense-a-closer-look?

www.operantcoffee.com/blog/2018/2/26/10-facts-about-the coffee-plant

www.motifcoffee.com/brew-your-best/coffee-fundamentals/about-
coffee-plant

www.operantcoffee.com/blog/2018/2/26/10-facts-about-the-coffee-plant

www.plentifulearth.com/coffee-magical-properties/

www.healthline.com/nutrition/uses-for-coffee-grounds#TOC_
  TITLE_HDR_4

www.speakingofwitchwands.net/2020/07/09/the-magickal-crape-
  myrtle-tree/

www.gardenguides.com/12492666-the-facts-about-a-crape-myrtle.html

www.finedininglovers.com/article/myrtle-z-26-things-know

About the Author

Kac Young has three doctorates: a PhD in Natural Health, an ND in Naturopathy and a DCH in Clinical Hypnotherapy. She is a licensed Religious Science Minister and a producer and director with over thirty years of experience in the television industry.

Kac has traveled extensively to experience firsthand and to study world religions, beliefs, methods, practices, and disciplines. Her life goal is to bring spiritual awareness to everyone, so they are able to live full, productive, generous lives and leave the world a better place for having been in it. She believes that every desire must be spiritually connected and consciously infused in order for change to transpire. When desire and intention meet passion and action, shift occurs. When shift occurs, change happens, and desired results are experienced.

To date she has written dozens of self-help books, including: *Heart Easy: The Food Lover's Guide to Heart Healthy Eating, Discover Your Spiritual Genius, Feng Shui the Easy Way, Dancing with the Moon, 21 Days to the Love of Your Life, Gold Mind, Cheese Dome Power, The Path to Fabulous, The Quick Guide to Bach Flower Remedies, Supreme Healing, The Enlightened Person's Guide to Raising a Dog, Chart Your Course, The Healing Art of Essential Oils, Essential Oils for Beginners, The One-Minute Cat Manager, Natural Healing for Cats Combining Bach Flower Remedies and Behavior Therapy, Beyond Beginning Crystals, The Art of Healing with Crystals, Crystal Power, 12 Essential Crystal for Health and Healing, Pendulum Power Wisdom and Healing, Living the Faerie Life*, and the annual *Essential Oils Wall Calendar* for Llewellyn Publishing (2020–2022).

Index

Mango Publishing, established in 2014, publishes an eclectic list of books by diverse authors—both new and established voices—on topics ranging from business, personal growth, women's empowerment, LGBTQ studies, health, and spirituality to history, popular culture, time management, decluttering, lifestyle, mental wellness, aging, and sustainable living. We were recently named 2019 *and* 2020's #1 fastest growing independent publisher by *Publishers Weekly*. Our success is driven by our main goal, which is to publish high quality books that will entertain readers as well as make a positive difference in their lives.

Our readers are our most important resource; we value your input, suggestions, and ideas. We'd love to hear from you—after all, we are publishing books for you!

Please stay in touch with us and follow us at:
Facebook: Mango Publishing
Twitter: @MangoPublishing
Instagram: @MangoPublishing
LinkedIn: Mango Publishing
Pinterest: Mango Publishing
Newsletter: mangopublishinggroup.com/newsletter

Join us on Mango's journey to reinvent publishing, one book at a time.

CPSIA information can be obtained
at www.ICGtesting.com
Printed in the USA
JSHW031317090522
25741JS00002B/108